D0992636

The Golf MasterMind®

The Golf MasterMind®

Plot Your Course
To
Better Golf

Rick Heard, PGA

Copyright © 2016 by Rick Heard

All rights reserved.

No part of this book – text or images – may be reproduced or utilized in any form or by any means, electronic or mechanical, including photocopying and recording, or by any information storage and retrieval system without permission in writing from Rick Heard.

Published by ARD Publishing
Boca Raton, Florida

Printed in the United States of America

Text and cover design by Rick Heard

Golf MasterMind® is a registered trademark of Rick Heard, PGA

 Like Golf MasterMind on facebook

ISBN: 0-9913557-2-5
ISBN-13: 978-0-9913557-2-3

To my Dad

CONTENTS

ACKNOWLEDGMENTS

I am thankful to many people who have encouraged me over the years, which led to me adding "author" to my suite of hats. He never knew it, but Mike Cushinsky probably started me on the path at my first job out of college. They were only memos and technical reports, but he sent me back to the keyboard more times than I want to admit.

I thank Diana Law, who years later when thinking of all of the teaching games we pros had created, she said "someone should write all of this down." I took the job. Then, when I began caddying for my son in junior golf tournaments, my books "Daddy Caddy on the Bag" and "Daddy Caddy Off the Bag" literally came to me almost overnight.

Now four years later, I am grateful to all those who have supported those books and their premise. Dan Van Horn of U.S. Kids Golf, Michelle Holmes, numerous PGA and LPGA pros, and countless "daddy caddies" have all pushed me to continue.

This book exists because the game of golf is demanding and it challenges us physically as well as mentally. I thank my parents for separating me from my golf clubs when I broke one of them in anger as a kid. I thank Steve Condore for showing me the grace of the recovery shot. I thank my wonderful wife for her patience and understanding as I burned the midnight oil. I thank Alex for the inspiration that led to the Golf MasterMind concept.

There are many books on the mental game of golf written by distinguished authors. Dr. Rick Jensen is one of the best. I am grateful to Dr. Rick for his willingness to review this book, for his time and suggestions, and for all that he has done to challenge the status quo and improve the world of golf instruction for us teaching professionals and our students.

And, I thank Don Law for trusting me and believing in me to create a new mental/emotional coaching system for our elite golf programs.

FOREWORD

By Dr. Rick Jensen, Ph.D.

The game of golf has certainly changed over the years – course conditions are much improved, rule changes have been introduced, and enhancements in ball and club design have helped players hit the ball farther and straighter than ever before. With all of these changes, the one aspect of the game that remains constant is the mental game. Today's players deal with the same mental challenges as did those competing in the era of Hogan and Snead. Pressure, distractions, slow play, slumps, nervousness, fear, water hazards, and more – all are inherent aspects of the game that challenge our mental toughness.

I recall a conversation that I had years ago with the esteemed Ken Venturi, winner of the 1964 U.S. Open, during which he said to me "During my day, we didn't have mental gurus like you to teach us the correct way to think and manage ourselves on the course. We had to learn mental toughness on our own through trial-and-error." Certainly, things have changed in this aspect of the game! Today's golfers have access to fantastic coaches and resources - like Rick Heard and his Golf MasterMind system. Rick not only teaches players the technical skills required for effective club delivery and ball control, but he integrates mental skill development into their training programs.

Rick's personal golf background as an accomplished player has provided him with keen insights into what it takes to play to your potential on the golf course. In The Golf MasterMind, Rick has combined his years of playing and coaching experience to provide you with a practical system through which you can develop your mental toughness. What is unique about the Golf MasterMind system is Rick's understanding and explanation of how your on-course performance is affected by both your ability to control the ball and your ability to manage your mind.

As a sport psychologist, I've had the opportunity to work with some of the game's top professionals on the PGA and LPGA Tours. Unquestionably, these players are mentally tough. More importantly, they are good! I often say to them "If you are not good, you will soon be mental." Like these great players, you too must recognize that there is an unbinding relationship between your acquired golf skills (driving, pitching, putting, etc.) and your mental toughness. If you are hitting balls out of bounds on every other hole, it is very difficult to remain focused, disciplined, and motivated to play good golf. As you will learn from Rick's discussion of his Peak Performance Pyramid, your ability is an essential dimension on your path to great golf.

The Golf MasterMind provides you with a roadmap to playing to your potential in the game of golf. Throughout the book, you will have the opportunity to reflect upon your game and assess your existing self-regulation skills. Furthermore, Rick will provide you with practical drills and strategies for improving the way you think and behave on the course. When it is all said and done, you will become a Golf MasterMind Pro.

Parkland, Florida

FROM THE AUTHOR

"Arrrrgh! I could have shot a great round today if only I had…" – you complete this exasperating sentence. How many times have you said it? I know I have said and heard it countless times. The usual response is to go back to the range to hit more balls. This book is not the usual response.

"The Golf MasterMind" takes a different approach to help you play to your potential. We all work hard on our swings and technique, and our ball-striking skills determine our potential. However, we frequently leave strokes on the course. I call this difference the "gap" between what is and what could be. Most of our practice and instruction focuses on improving our physical skills… yet most of the gap is explained by a combination of ball-striking skills and mental and emotional skills. The Golf MasterMind system aims to help you reduce your gap by taking a holistic approach to improving both your outer and inner game.

The Golf MasterMind concept grew out of my work as a PGA teaching professional, golf coach, author, and lector. Sports psychology, particularly the mental and emotional game of golf, has been a passion of mine for years. When my partners Don Law, Diana Law, Jennifer Moss, and I decided to expand the Don Law Golf Academy to include full-time students and a peak performance training program, I saw the opportunity to formalize my thinking into a comprehensive golf mental game coaching system. I emphasize that it is a system, rather than a stand-alone program, because the physical, mental, and emotional aspects of golf must be integrated into everything you do if you want to make the most of your golf talents.

Little did I know it, but the seeds of this system were sown in my book "Daddy Caddy on the Bag," written four years ago to help parents manage the challenging job of parenting and coaching their young golfers and bringing out the best in their children through golf. In "Daddy Caddy on the Bag," I first proposed the idea of the Peak Performance Pyramid and discussed, in a cursory way, my keys to the mental game.

Now, in developing a comprehensive mental game system for our elite golfers, I have expanded on these topics and created the concept of the "Golf MasterMind." My thinking behind this fancy sounding name is simple: In order to accomplish anything, you first have to want to do it. Then, you have to be able to do it. Then, you have to figure out how to do it, focus on getting it done, and believe that you can do it. When those elements are in place, almost anything is possible.

A Golf MasterMind is a golfer who makes the most of his or her physical golf abilities through the use of superior self management skills. I believe there are five dimensions that are measurable and which complement one another to describe any golfer's position on the Golf MasterMind scale. These are motivation, ability, strategy, focus, and confidence.

This book describes each of these and the overall Golf MasterMind concept in detail, with the objective of helping you play better golf. The book explains how these elements interrelate, and includes practical worksheets, evaluations, and drills to allow you to assess your position and improve on each level. Along the way, you will find the answers to these three questions:

1. What is a Golf MasterMind?
2. Where are you on the Golf MasterMind rating scale?
3. What can you do to become a Golf MasterMind Pro?

In some ways, the answers to these questions are personal and unique to each golfer. Much of this topic requires personal thought, introspection, self-discovery, and enlightenment.

Written for golfers of all abilities, the aim is to help everyone play the best they can play given their existing physical skills. Although this book is about golf, the Golf MasterMind concept can be applied to almost everything you do in life – other sports, schoolwork, business, your career, even your personal relationships. This may all sound like a lot of work, but it can also be a lot of fun and could be a life-changing experience.

I hope you enjoy the journey!

INTRODUCTION

"Competitive golf is played mainly on a 5-and-a-half inch course… the space between your ears."

— Bobby Jones

The Golf MasterMind

My dictionary defines a "mastermind" as "a highly intelligent person, especially one who plans or plots and directs a complex or difficult project, such as the mastermind of a robbery." High-level competitive golf is surely complex and difficult, and playing the game well certainly requires a degree of planning and plotting your way around the course. Moreover, golfers need to be able to master their emotions and their state of mind through the various challenges and situations that arise in the course of play.

This line of thinking led me to develop the concept of the "Golf MasterMind" – someone who can make the most of their talents and skills and "plot their course to better golf." However, I was never intending to equate golf with bank robbery!

The Golf MasterMind concept is designed to help you play better golf – that is, shoot lower scores. As you work on your physical golf game through lessons and practice, you will see improvement in ball striking, short game, putting, and every facet of your ability to hit a golf ball. However, those things alone do not guarantee a lower score, and they certainly don't ensure that you will play your best in tournament conditions or under pressure.

The Golf MasterMind concept combines your physical outer game with your inner game. Golf MasterMind is about your ability to manage your thoughts and emotions so that you use your physical game to the best of your abilities and minimize what I call the "gap." By "gap," I mean the difference between your actual score and your potential score. Your physical golf skills and abilities determine your potential score. Your mental golf ability – your "inner game" – is the factor that determines whether or not you will play to your potential.

The Golf MasterMind concept and the importance of the inner game can be demonstrated by watching PGA or LPGA Tour pros on a tournament day. On the range or practice areas, virtually all tour pros look like ball-striking robots, each hitting perfect shot after perfect shot. It is truly amazing to sit in the stands or watch near the practice areas and see how consistent they all are at hitting balls. Anyone watching them would rightly assume that each pro would shoot under par every time they tee it up, and surely that is their potential.

However, the reality of their golf scores is quite different. What explains the difference in their scores? They all have immense talent and the capability to hit nearly every type of golf shot under nearly every condition. Although there are some differences in their physical games (such as distance off the tee), these differences don't fully explain the variation in scores.

Certainly a big explanatory factor is each pro's consistency and ability to minimize the frequency and severity of mis-hits. However, I believe the greatest explanatory factor is the mind, or how each pro uses his or her physical talents and abilities when it matters, under pressure, in tournament conditions on the course. Those who understand that they will make some mistakes and can accept those errors and move on and remain focused, and who are Golf MasterMind Pros are the ones who make the most of their physical skills and consistently play to their potential.

Truly, your mental golf management skills are the "15th club" in your bag. They are your secret weapon that will help you score better than your competitors. Skilled golfers practice to hone all aspects of their physical game: putting, chipping, bunker shots, approach shots, driving, trouble shots, and more. Champion golfers also work hard to sharpen their mental and emotional skills.

As such, the Golf MasterMind approach should be integrated into everything you do as you work to improve your game. The Golf MasterMind concept begins with an in-depth understanding of your physical ball-striking and ball control abilities. Golf MasterMind also incorporates best practices in the complex field of sports psychology, using HeartMath as its core science for emotional control. The system provides a framework to guide each golfer, but is flexible to recognize the unique needs of each person.

What Is a Golf Mastermind?

A Golf MasterMind is someone who makes the most of his or her golf abilities through focus, intelligent decision making, mental toughness, strategic thinking, and emotional control. Anyone can be a Golf MasterMind – it has nothing to do with your golf swing, how far you hit the ball, or the quality of your short game. Rather, it has everything to do with how you <u>use</u> your physical golf talents – whatever they are. Being a Golf MasterMind is about being the best that you can be when it matters. It is about playing your best, whatever your personal best is. It is about playing to your potential whether it is in the heat of tournament competition or under the pressure of a weekly $2 nassau with your golf buddies.

The Golf MasterMind framework is based on the following five components that complement one another and together build toward peak golf performance:

1. **Motivation** – Peak performance begins with motivation, which is driven by inspiration, desire, dedication, and dreams… the drive to do what is necessary to learn and improve and achieve your fullest potential. Motivation comes from the inner drive to set and achieve goals that are lofty, yet reasonable and achievable. Motivation is the foundation of performance and becoming a Golf MasterMind, because without motivation, your potential will never be achieved. Motivation also includes the concept of resilience, which is a key part of your mental toughness and your ability to handle pressure, setbacks, and failure and still keep reaching to achieve your goals.

2. **Ability** – Ability is the combination of talent and skill that you possess and that can be developed through self-discovery, practice, and instruction. You may think of ability as only being your physical ability to hit a golf ball, but a Golf MasterMind also has the ability to control himself or herself. Therefore, ability includes both ball control and self management. Ability can be thought of as a limiting factor: your ball-striking ability sets the limit on how

low your scores can potentially go. Your Golf MasterMind ability sets the limit on how low your scores will <u>actually</u> go; that is, whether or not you will use your physical talents to the best of your ability.

3. **Strategy** – I think of strategy as how well you know your own game and how you use your golf ability to navigate the golf course. A Golf MasterMind knows his or her capabilities and limitations, and has no ego when it comes to dissecting a golf course. Strategy requires that you know something about golf course design and how the course should be played. It also requires that you know your own strengths and weaknesses so that you can develop the best plan of attack for every hole and make good decisions… for <u>you</u>.

4. **Focus** – Golf is unique among sports in part because it requires us to focus intently on the task when it is time to hit our golf ball, then it requires that we relax and somehow pass the time during long intervals between shots. It is impossible for anyone to remain focused on the essential parts of playing golf for the entire four to five hours it takes to play 18 holes. Focus also includes emotional control and your ability to accept errors and mistakes on the golf course. Therefore, a Golf MasterMind has the ability to accept what happened in the past and turn his or her focus on when needed, then turn it off between shots.

5. **Confidence** – The final component of peak performance is confidence, or the unshakable belief in your own ability to perform. As a Golf MasterMind, you remain optimistic and know that you can achieve those lofty motivational goals; that you have the physical and mental ability to perform according to your strategic plan of attack, and that you can focus in the heat of the moment when the shot matters the most.

I like to represent these building blocks in the form of a pyramid, because it helps show how the components relate to each other. As with a building, it helps to have a solid foundation and sound construction so that the higher levels of our performance have solid support. I call this the "Peak Performance Pyramid"

The Peak Performance Pyramid

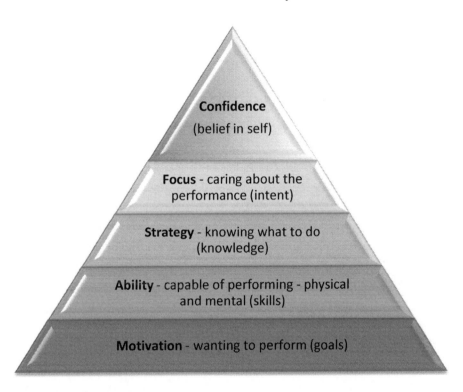

As an example, the pyramid concept clearly shows that everything you hope to achieve in golf depends on your degree of motivation. Just saying that your goal is to play college golf, for example, is meaningless if you don't have the burning inner desire to put in the practice work, suffer the setbacks and inevitable failures, and persevere over the long term to get there.

And, although you may have this intense motivation, you must also have the physical ball-striking abilities and mental abilities to think strategically and remain coherent and focused in the heat of competition. Even with all of this, you must also have the confidence that you can put the pieces together and succeed.

Clearly, this is not a simple task for anyone, especially for young golfers! However, as I said above, anyone can be a Golf MasterMind, and you are already *somewhere* on the Golf MasterMind scale. I think of this as your "altitude" on the Peak Performance Pyramid.

Organization of this Book

As introduced above, the Golf MasterMind concept is based on the five key factors of Motivation, Ability, Strategy, Focus, and Confidence that all work together to help you be the best that you can be. These factors are depicted as levels of the Peak Performance Pyramid.

The following five chapters discuss each of these levels in detail, and explain the rationale and purpose of each level. There are multiple worksheets, evaluations, and surveys that will help you measure your progress as you climb the Peak Performance Pyramid and plot your course toward being a Golf MasterMind Pro. Use them often to monitor your progress as you improve both your physical golf skills and your mental Golf MasterMind abilities.

I am confident that if you follow this process in concert with some assistance and direction from your PGA or LPGA teaching professional, you will make a significant and lasting improvement in your game.

The final chapter on being a Golf MasterMind Pro has a brief survey questionnaire for each level. Taken together with the worksheets introduced in the first five chapters, these tools will provide the following:

- A dreams / goals / objectives document that will guide your progress.

- An inner game Gap Analysis to help you understand lost/wasted strokes.

- A Skills Evaluation Worksheet to measure your physical golf skills.

- A Carry Distance Worksheet to help you understand your capabilities.

- A "Focus-ability" Scorecard to measure how well you focus.

- An understanding of your position on each level of the Pyramid.

- An assessment of your mental toughness quotient.

- Your overall Golf MasterMind rating.

Blank copies of all of the worksheets are included in Appendix 1. A series of fun golf practice games that can help you target improvement in specific skill areas are included in Appendix 2.

I have also developed a Golf MasterMind Workbook to accompany this book. The Workbook contains instructions and blank worksheets for all of the Golf MasterMind evaluations and surveys.

Lastly, my golfmastermindpro.com website contains more information and electronic versions of the worksheets and surveys for your convenience (website membership required).

The rest is up to you!

CHAPTER ONE

"Always make a total effort, even when the odds are against you."

– Arnold Palmer

Motivation

I believe that you can accomplish almost anything that you want to accomplish. Whether it is your choice of careers, learning to play an instrument, or your desire to improve your golf game, you can do it. If you truly want to do it. When you want something badly enough, you will be motivated to make it happen. It will be something that you dream about, something that inspires you, and that you dedicate yourself to accomplishing. You will "move mountains" to achieve your dream. Nothing will stand in your way, including failures, setbacks, naysayers, and struggles. You only need motivation.

But where do you find it?

You can't just decide to do something and hope that it happens. And you surely can't accomplish something that you don't really want to do. You find motivation deep inside your soul when you search within and discover who you really want to be and what you really want to do.

I know this may sound overly philosophical or spiritual, and it might seem like overkill to apply this thinking to your golf game, but it is true. It is one thing to *say* that you want to improve your golf scores, or that you want to win a tournament or earn a college scholarship. It is an entirely different thing to have the inner drive to do it.

Motivation is the foundation of virtually everything we do, and certainly it is the foundation of sports performance.

But what is motivation?

Motivation is a psychological concept that can be expressed in a cycle, as shown below:

Golf MasterMind Motivational Cycle

Where does motivation come from? There are many theories of motivation, and it is a fascinating human behavior topic. Here is how I think it works:

You can be motivated either externally or internally. External motivation is where someone or something else is encouraging you to improve your golf game. Internal motivation is where you yourself want to improve your golf game. There is an enormous difference between these two scenarios. You might try to accomplish something that someone else wants you to do, but you probably won't give it your all. Ultimately, you may think to yourself "I don't want to do what *they* want me to do… I want to do what *I* want to do." You need to be self-motivated.

Furthermore, there are two types of internal motivation. One is where you are pushing yourself to improve your golf game because you want to play better, or perhaps to win a tournament or earn a scholarship. The other is where your dream or goal is so strong that it is pulling you toward it. Pull motivation is where you can't put down the book because you just have to see how it ends. Pull motivation is where you fall head over heels in love and you have an unquenchable burning desire to see that person again. Pull motivation is where you imagine yourself putting to win the U.S. Open and that vision is embedded in your soul, and you can't wait for another chance to practice and improve.

If your internal motivation is push, you will push yourself as hard as possible to achieve your dream. However, you must be wary of setbacks and failures that might convince you that your dream is not achievable.

If your internal motivation is pull, you will feel yourself falling almost helplessly toward your dreams and goals. Setbacks and failures will be but bumps in the road on your way to achievement.

Regardless of which type of motivation you believe you have, you must ultimately be driven by a deep internal desire to accomplish your dreams.

We often speak of motivation in elite athletes in such terms as "the will to win," the "it" factor, and "grit." These are our attempts to give names to that intangible inner drive that is motivation.

Motivation is the foundation of the Peak Performance Pyramid because it is the force that will drive you to succeed. Without motivation, great talent and skill can be wasted. With motivation, hidden talent can be exposed and skills can be developed that far surpass expectations.

As an example, I think the world of golfers can be divided into three groups. First, there is the group of what I call "phenomenal phenoms." These are golfers who were phenomenal young golfers. They were the best at their club, in their city, or in their school. They were top players who were seen as the "next big name." And they followed through and became phenomenal professional golfers. When I ask people to think of a "phenomenal phenom," Tiger Woods always comes to mind. However, it is difficult to think of many more, and indeed there are not many.

I call the second group "phenomenal no-names." Like the first group, these are people who were phenomenal young golfers, seemingly destined for greatness. They dominated their golf world. They were virtually unbeatable, and there seemed to be no way they could fail to make it on the PGA Tour or LPGA Tour.

But then, they disappeared.

For whatever reason, they dropped out of the elite golf world. This doesn't mean that they are not great and successful people; just that they didn't capitalize on their golf abilities. But why?

I have seen many young golfers like this, and now fully grown, they still have amazing golf skills and endless talent. Those things didn't go away – you can't "lose" talent or forget how to swing a club. What went away was their golf motivation. Whether from burnout, frustration, or the myriad other things that competed for their attention, they just lost sight of their golf dreams and goals. Sadly, they failed to capitalize on their extraordinary golf talent, and directed their energies in other directions.

In some ways, I think "phenomenal no-names" fail to make it *because of* their phenomenal talent and skill. Such early talent can easily lead to complacency, where young athletes can dominate their sport without really trying too hard. Their natural athletic ability allows them to succeed against others who aren't as gifted. This complacency can lead to poor practice and work habits and a lack of motivation. When this happens, the phenoms can find themselves suddenly overtaken by others and, without the inner drive and motivation, may simply give up and move on to other activities.

Raw talent can only take you so far, and then some amount of work is required to excel at an elite level. Perhaps "phenomenal no-names" are too accustomed to succeeding the easy way, and never have the motivation to put in the hard work necessary to make the most of their talent.

Then there is the third group. The world of golf also has many of what I call "no-name phenoms." These are people who didn't even play golf at a young age, or if they did they were, in the words of 2015 FedEx Cup Champion Billy Horschel, "nothing special." Many of them were multi-sport athletes who didn't decide to specialize in golf until they were in their teens. Others simply were introduced to the game at a later age. No matter how it happened, when they found golf, they fell in love with the game and it became their passion. Their boundless internal motivation drove them to succeed, often in spite of less than perfect practice facilities, limited access to golf courses, a lack of formal instruction, and even a lack of natural talent.

Indeed, these "no-name phenoms" persevered against the odds, letting nothing stop them from reaching their dreams. Guided by their dreams, they overcame all obstacles with hard work and determination. A Golf MasterMind Pro has this level of motivation, and it will propel you to success in everything you do.

As you think about these three groups of people, remember that these groups are described only by their golf accomplishments, and that they all are "phenoms" in some way. All have been excellent golfers at some point in their lives. And, they all are good people whether or not they stay with golf as a profession, become successful at business, or pursue other endeavors.

Which type of phenom are you?

The Keys to Motivation

Here are the key components of the foundation of the Peak Performance Pyramid, motivation:

1. Dreams
2. Goals and Objectives
3. Mental Toughness

The following sections will explore each of these in detail.

Dreams

What is your dream? Is it to play on the PGA Tour or the LPGA Tour? Is it to get a college scholarship? Perhaps it is to play well enough to compete in top amateur tournaments. Or, it might be to enjoy social and business golf with friends and associates. Some people might simply have the dream of being able to play any golf course without being embarrassed.

It doesn't matter what your dream is… it is only important that you have one. Your dream will provide that guiding light that will keep you moving in the right direction, and provide inspiration that will keep you focused on moving forward. Here is an example:

I know a boy who was watching a golf tournament on TV with his dad. When the telecast was over, the boy looked up and said "I want to be a professional golfer." He was only five years old at the time and had never played golf. His parents, also non golfers, were incredulous but got him started with a few clubs. Six months later, he told his kindergarten teacher that he was going to win the Masters someday. This amazing motivation led to a set of golf clubs, thousands of practice balls, endless hours on the driving range, and dozens of successful junior tournaments. Now, five years later, the boy still sees himself putting to win the Masters one day, and that dream still powers his motivation to be a champion golfer.

The surest way to achieve your dreams and succeed in anything is to possess the burning inner desire to succeed. Obviously, more things are also needed, and these will be discussed under the remaining levels of the Peak Performance Pyramid. However, this intense desire lets nothing get in your way, and guides you through difficult times, setbacks, and failures. Golf and life are both full of these roadblocks, and you must see your way through these obstacles and continue to drive toward your dream.

But what is it that you really want to achieve? You may or may not be aware of your dreams, and you may not have truly thought through the depths of what you ultimately want to accomplish.

Now is the time for you to give some sincere thought to the following questions:

- Why do you play golf?
  o What do you really want?

- What are your dreams for the future?
  o What do you hope to achieve?

     o   What do you see yourself doing?
     o   Where do you see yourself in:
- 10 years?
- 5 years?
- 1 year?

- What can you do to make these dreams a reality?

- What roadblocks are potentially in your way?
  - What can you do about them?
  - What can others do to help clear the way?

Ultimately, you are the only person who is responsible for your success. Others, including your parents, other family members, mentors, teachers, coaches, and friends can help you by enabling or encouraging you, but you must take ownership and responsibility. Once you have given these questions some thought, it is time to get specific.

Goals and Objectives

If your dream is your ultimate destination, then your goals are major stops along the way that once achieved, continue to move you in the right direction. Goals are long on direction, but short on specifics, without worrying about how they will be accomplished.

For example, you can set a goal to break 80 without having a specific plan as to how to do it. Your goals keep you focused by allowing you to achieve short term successes as you continue to move forward toward your dream.

Perhaps the most important part of this process is for you to establish challenging yet reasonable goals. "Challenging" means that your goals will not be easy to reach. "Reasonable" means that your goals, though challenging, *are* reachable. Just as it is of no use to set goals that are virtually unattainable, it is pointless to set goals that can be reached with little effort. Moreover, it is critical that these are *your* goals that you own for yourself. Remember, it doesn't matter what anyone else wants. It is your life, your future, and your choice to accomplish something.

Once you establish your goals, you can define your objectives. These are smaller steps that get more specific with a plan of attack that will help you achieve your goals. If goals are about the big picture, then objectives are all about tactics and "how-to," or action plans to get from where you are to where you want to be.

Keeping with the above example goal of breaking 80, your objectives would outline a specific set of actions that you will take to get there. These could include weekly swing instruction, short game lessons, a practice plan, and timelines for accomplishing each objective. Also, objectives can be "process" objectives. For example, although you cannot always control the outcome, you can usually control the process. This means you could set an objective to follow a certain routine or process that you use, such as "take a deep breath and visualize my target before stepping up to the ball."

Even if you don't achieve your scoring goal, you can achieve your process objectives. These show steady improvement in doing those things that will ultimately lead to your accomplishing your scoring goal.

Then, you must put your goals and objectives in writing. There is some sort of magic that happens when you commit your goals to paper that makes them take on a life of their own and that pushes you to amazing accomplishments. Your goals and objectives should be listed clearly, with realistic timeframes for achieving them.

Use the Golf MasterMind Goals worksheet in Appendix 1 to write your goals and objectives and timelines, and place them in a prominent place in your room or home so that you see them every day. Feel free to rearrange the worksheet or to add more room for information as needed. However, you are strongly encouraged to keep your goals and objectives simple and clear. Following the concepts outlined by George T. Doran in 1981 and widely used by Peter Drucker, your goals should be **S-M-A-R-T,** meaning they should be:

Specific – they should be well-defined and clear so that it is easy to know when you have achieved them.

Measurable – your goals should be precise and easy to measure. An example would be "break par for 18 holes."

Attainable – there is no point in setting a goal that you have no hope of achieving. Make your goals challenging, but keep them realistic.

Relevant – keep your goals aligned with the direction you want to go, and keep them focused to help you stay focused.

Time-bound – always attach a time limit or deadline for your goals. When you have a deadline to meet, your sense of urgency increases and you will achieve your goals much faster.

Here is an example (the blank worksheet is in Appendix 1):

Reaching for My Dream: My Golf MasterMind Golf Goals		
Goal **What I want to Achieve**	**Objective** **Steps I Can Take to Achieve My Goal**	**By When**
Break par in a competitive round this year	Practice short game 1 hour per day	ongoing
	Use HeartMath to improve my emotional control	End of August
	Refine my yardage charts to show realistic carry yardages with all of my irons	June 5

Once you have written your goals and objectives and dates for achieving them, you can begin taking action. This can include almost anything that gets you moving in the right direction. You only need to take small steps; do not feel like you have to accomplish everything all at once. It is more important that you are making progress and moving towards your goals.

Lastly, your goals and objectives should be flexible and fluid enough to change as you accomplish them. As you make progress, do not hesitate to review your goals and update them as needed.

Use the Golf MasterMind Goals form in Appendix 1 or the Golf MasterMind Workbook to get started, or use a form of your own. If you aren't comfortable with this form, feel free to begin with a blank sheet of paper. The format is not important. What is important is that you commit your dreams, goals and objectives to paper and begin to do things that will make them a reality.

Mental Toughness

Your dreams, goals and objectives are meaningless unless you are tough enough to persevere through the inevitable difficult times, failures, setbacks, and challenges that will occur. In order to survive these and other challenges, you must be mentally tough. But, what does that mean?

The concept of mental toughness is perhaps one of the least understood yet most studied concepts in sports psychology. What is it that makes one athlete fight with all of his or her soul, recover from setbacks and keep trying, while another (perhaps even more skilled) athlete succumbs to those very same setbacks and gives up?

The answer to this question can be highly personal and unique to each of us. To help you try to discover and enhance your own mental toughness, you must first define what mental toughness means to you. Second, you must train to strengthen your mental toughness. Fortunately, mental toughness can be enhanced through training!

Although there is no single common definition of mental toughness, researchers and elite coaches have identified mental toughness as one of the most important elements of peak performance. These experts agree on the major components of mental toughness, which include:

- Hardiness – endurance and physical strength.

- Perseverance and Persistence – sticking to a purpose or goal and never giving up.

- Resilience – the power of recovering quickly from setbacks and failures.

- Competitive Desire – the will to win.

- Dedication – willingness to work toward achieving goals and objectives.

Golf mental toughness is the psychological edge that allows you to consistently shoot scores commensurate with your skill level regardless of the conditions. A mentally tough golfer will find a way to grind out his or her best score in spite of setbacks, bad breaks, competitive pressure, challenging conditions, fatigue, and virtually any difficult situation.

And then, faced with all of the challenges inherent in the game of golf, a mentally tough golfer is able to bounce back from adversity and continue trying, even against the odds of success. This ability to recover from setbacks, called resilience, may indeed be the most important component of golf mental toughness, since competition does not allow for every golfer to experience success all of the time.

Mentally tough golfers have a strong desire to compete because they do not get discouraged and they keep on striving to be successful in competition. This attribute is critical in golf, because golfers may see themselves as "losers" if they don't win, even though stroke play golf isn't a win-lose event (1 winner and 1 loser). Yes, the winner wins, but the remaining players aren't "losers."

A mentally tough golfer has the burning inner desire and strength to persevere against all odds to excel. He or she has the physical and mental ability to consistently perform at his or her level of skill. He or she possesses the wisdom to play to his or her strengths and weaknesses to do what it takes to make the best score. He or she remains focused on long-term goals in the face of short-term setbacks, and has an unshakable belief in his or her ability to succeed.

NCAA Coaches Survey

In his doctoral dissertation, John Wayne Creasy, Phd., explored the attributes of mental toughness and surveyed NCAA coaches on the topic. The coaches prioritized their top 12 factors of mental toughness according to their value and importance to the elite college athlete.

These attributes are listed below, along with my suggestions in italics for how you can train to improve on each to develop and enhance your golf mental toughness.

NCAA Coaches' Mental Toughness Attributes

1. Having an unshakable self-belief in your ability to achieve your competition goals; and

2. Having an unshakable self-belief that you possess unique qualities and abilities that make you better than your opponents.

   These two attributes are a combination of confidence and ability, and can be enhanced by improving your golf skills, including ball control, decision making, and self management. In other words, in order for you to have confidence in and believe in your abilities, you have to demonstrate the necessary level of skill. Identifying your strengths and your opportunities for improvement will help build self-trust that you can perform in the heat of competition. The pressure of competition and general course conditions will cause the weakest skill areas to break down. Your golf training must identify and focus on strengthening these weak links so they don't break under pressure and to give you confidence in your abilities. NCAA coaches want golfers who have a balanced skill set, who work tenaciously to improve their weak links, and who have confidence in their abilities.

NCAA Coaches' Mental Toughness Attributes

3. Having an insatiable desire and internalized motives to succeed;

4. Bouncing back from performance setbacks as a result of increased determination to succeed; and

5. Thriving on the pressure of competition.

These three attributes are elements of motivation, which includes resilience. As described above, motivation can be developed by identifying your dreams, goals, and objectives. These frame your purpose and provide the internal drive for you to achieve success. NCAA coaches want golfers with that burning inner fire that will power them through difficult times and keep them focused on success. Golf mental toughness requires a high degree of resilience, since so much of the game is about managing and making the most of our mistakes. NCAA coaches want the golfer who becomes stronger and more determined after setbacks. The best way to train to improve these attributes is to play challenging practice games that simulate actual play and which provide opportunities to fail and recover.

NCAA Coaches' Mental Toughness Attributes

6. Accepting that competition anxiety is inevitable and knowing that you can cope with it;

7. Not being adversely affected by others' good and bad performances;

8. Remaining fully-focused in the face of personal life distractions;

9. Switching a sport focus on and off as required; and

10. Remaining fully focused on the task at hand in the face of competition-specific distractions.

These five are all elements of focus, which could be more critical for golf than many other sports. NCAA coaches want the golfer who can remain focused on golf in spite of the myriad distractions of college life. They want the golfer who channels competition anxiety in a productive way to play better. They value the golfer who can wear "blinkers" and ignore what their fellow-competitors are doing and remain focused on their own game. And, they want the golfer who can relax between shots, but "flip the switch" and focus intently on each shot as required. As before, the best way to train to improve these attributes is to play challenging practice games and matches that simulate the pressure of actual competition situations, complete with artificial distractions as desired.

NCAA Coaches' Mental Toughness Attributes

11. Pushing back the boundaries of physical and emotional pain, while still maintaining technique and effort under distress (in training and competition).

    This attribute is a mix of motivation, ability, and focus. NCAA coaches want golfers who persevere through long and challenging practice sessions and physical and emotional stress, maintaining their form and concentration during difficult times. Again, realistic practice games and matches can help strengthen these attributes by subjecting golfers to real and simulated conditions that could cause one of the weak links to break.

12. Regaining psychological control following unexpected, uncontrollable events.

    *This final attribute is an element of focus, particularly emotional control and anger management. NCAA coaches want the golfer who understands that bad breaks, poor swings, bad bounces, and external events such as severe weather conditions are simply a part of the game. These and many other similar events **will** happen. The mentally tough golfer will accept these roadblocks, deal with the situation calmly and move on, leaving them in the past and not letting their memory affect his or her next shot. As before, the best way to train for this is to simulate these conditions in structured practice games and activities. The more difficult these simulations are, the easier it will be to deal with the real events that occur on the golf course when it counts.*

•   •   •

Motivation is the foundation of virtually everything we do, and it supplies the power for us to forge through difficult times, setbacks, and challenges. Driven by dreams, goals, and objectives, a Golf MasterMind will plot his or her way through those obstacles with a long-term view of success.

Perhaps the most important component of motivation is mental toughness and resilience, the ability to bounce back from the inevitable failures that golf is sure to provide. Without this toughness, goals and dreams are meaningless. With motivation and mental toughness, almost any dream can be achieved.

CHAPTER TWO

"Much of the difference between golfers can be explained by the gap between what could be and what is. Mind the gap!"

- Rick Heard

Ability

The second level of the Peak Performance Pyramid is ability. Your ability to control your golf ball and your ability to control yourself are the next most important keys following motivation. It is one thing to have the inner burning desire and endless motivation to become a better golfer. It is another thing to have the physical and mental ability to realistically do it. Therefore, in this chapter we will explore your physical and mental ability to play golf.

It is obvious that your golf scores are dependent on your ability to play the game. The better you can swing your club, the better you can hit the ball. The more skill you have, the better you can control your distance, trajectory, spin, etc. The better you are at putting, the more putts you will make.

These skills are evidence of your physical ability, and are the parts of you the golfer that everyone can see. But there is another, hidden part of you that only you can see, and it is your inner golfer. This is not a book about the golf swing or swing mechanics, nor is it a book about becoming a Zen golfer. However, it is critical that you be able to manage your inner golf skills if you are to become a Golf MasterMind Pro.

This chapter on ability introduces the inner game concept of your "gap" (I'll explain in a moment), and sets the stage for those following chapters as they dive deeper into the elements of the Golf MasterMind system. Chapter three of this book is about strategy, or choosing the best way to attack the golf course based on your own game. Chapter four is about focus, which requires that you "flip the switch" and concentrate on the shot you are about to hit. Chapter five is about confidence, to clear your mind of doubts about your ability to hit the shot you are about to attempt.

However, we must first set the baseline on your physical skills, since virtually all of your inner game abilities require that you have an intimate and realistic knowledge of your physical game, the types of shots you are capable of hitting, and your strengths and weaknesses, i.e., your outer game.

For these reasons, this chapter on ability is focused on the two facets of your game: your outer, physical game and your inner mental game. The outer game is all about swing mechanics, ball striking, scoring, types of shots, putts, and all of those things that any spectator could see. Your outer game determines your potential; that is it sets the limit on how low your scores could realistically go.

For example, if you can only hit your driver 150 yards and you are playing a 6,500 yard golf course, you simply can't expect to break 80. Your potential score (think of it as your "personal par") will be around 90. That limit is set by your limited ability to drive the ball far enough to have realistic chances at birdies and pars. Similarly, if you are not able to hit your ball within 20 feet of the hole reliably on your approach shots, you can't expect to make many birdies. Likewise, if you have trouble chipping to within five feet of the hole, you can't expect to save par most of the time. All of the characteristics of your outer game combine to determine your potential. I'll address your outer game and your physical skills in a moment, but first, let's look at your inner game.

Inside Your Golf Brain – the Inner Game

Your inner game is all about you and those things that only you know about yourself and your golf game. These are things that only you can see and feel. Your inner game ability determines whether you will play to your potential or not.

For example, if you possess the ball-striking abilities of a Tour player, you have the physical potential to break par. However, if you aren't able to manage your inner game and you don't have the ability to select the proper shot (strategy), use your pre-shot and post-shot routines (focus), and believe that you can hit the chosen shot (confidence), then you will not score to your potential. Instead of breaking par, you will shoot a "solid" 75, and go home thinking of a dozen ways you could have saved strokes, and how you "should have shot a 68."

Or, perhaps you are a weekend golfer who plays for fun. You don't practice too much, but you are capable of hitting many good shots. From the proper tees, your potential might be to play bogey golf, but you shot a 95. Just like the tour-caliber player, you can think of a dozen ways you could have shot an 88. In other words, your score itself doesn't really matter. It's the difference that counts.

This difference between your actual and your potential score is what I call the "gap," and it is where you have the best opportunity to improve your game right now. When it comes to scoring, our mistakes, mis-hits, and mental errors lie in the gap. This gap is the focus of the Golf MasterMind concept and it is where you can save strokes almost immediately. You will probably never find some magical golf swing tip that will make an immediate improvement in your physical outer game that will lower your potential score.

It is ironic that we always look to our outer game for improvement. Whether it is a tip from a magazine, a television show, a book, or a friend, we are all quick to listen and try out the "new swing" the next time on the golf course. Predictably, these tips usually don't work, or if they do, they don't last. I'm not against lessons and working on your physical skills and swing mechanics – after all, I am a PGA teaching professional. However, these things alone often don't yield immediate results, and any long term changes in your scoring potential from these will be incremental.

However, in your quest to be a Golf MasterMind Pro, you will find many ways in which you can sharpen your inner game and shrink the gap between what is and what could be. Most of us have a large gap of anywhere from five to ten strokes in a typical round. I often think that if I were to caddie for my students, I could save them ten strokes per round. Since I'm not there to be your caddie, how can you do this on your own?

One of the first such ways is to realize and accept that you have a gap, and to embrace it. I almost hesitate to recommend this, because golf is such a challenging game and the gap concept seems negative at first. Although you may play quite well and hit many excellent shots during a round, golf is replete with errors in judgment, poor decisions, and poor swings. It can appear negative to focus on just the mistakes, and in fact we do need to always find the joy in our great shots, par saves, and birdies.

However, the gap is there for all of us. As Ben Hogan said, "A good round of golf is if you can hit about three shots that turn out exactly as you planned them." All the others are misses. The point is to make those misses good enough. As Hogan also said, "This is a game of misses. The guy who misses the best is going to win."

You may think that this is a negative, pessimistic approach, but I think the opposite. I'm an eternal optimist, and I think about my rounds and my gap in a positive way. I think over my round and look at what could have been, replaying shots in my head, giving myself credit for shots that turned out well, thinking of the shots I could have played differently, and finding all of those strokes I could have saved. Not only does this calculate my gap for the round, but it helps me refine my approach for future rounds by helping me recognize potential errors so I can hope to avoid making them the next time on the course.

As an example, one of our young elite players recently finished second in an important junior tournament. He shot 1-over par for the 36-hole event and finished one stroke behind the winner, but he quickly told me how he had quadruple bogeyed a par 3 in his final round. "What happened on the quad?" I asked. He had been in thick bushes near the green on a par 3, and instead of calling his ball unplayable and going back to the tee (there were no playable drop options from his ball), he tried to hack the ball out, taking four shots to get his ball on the green only a few yards away. That poor decision probably cost him the tournament, not counting any of the other less costly mistakes he made over the course of the 36 holes.

Of course, it didn't seem to him like a poor choice at the time. In fact, he was certain that the poor choice would have been to return to the tee. Surely he thought he could get his ball closer to the hole with two swings from here than he could by going back to the tee and hitting his third shot. He was wrong. Hopefully, he will remember this the next time he finds himself in a similar situation.

I find it fascinating that we all have a gap, and it varies from round to round and from player to player. My young friend's gap for the tournament was about 8 strokes, meaning his potential was to shoot 7-under par for the event. The young man who won that tournament by a single stroke also had a gap, but perhaps his gap was smaller. I'm sure he also could have saved several strokes over the 36 holes. Perhaps his potential score for the tournament was 2-under, but his gap was only 2 strokes and he shot even par. As Hogan implied, that guy missed the best.

The nature of golf is that we always think about what could have been when we finish our round. In my life of thousands of rounds of golf, I can remember only a few where I left the 18th green knowing that I didn't leave any strokes out there. Most of the time, we leave those strokes (the gap) on the course due to mental errors or breakdowns of some sort, not due to poor swing mechanics. These mental errors include strategic errors, lack of focus, loss of emotional control, and lack of confidence – all things that are part of being a Golf MasterMind.

So, as a first step to getting in touch with your inner game, you should make it a ritual to think about your own gap following every round, and categorize the lost strokes such as this:

- Wrong strategy (e.g., you should have hit a layup shot instead of going for the green; you hit for a tucked hole location instead of playing for the middle of the green, etc.). These might have occurred because you didn't know the golf course, or perhaps you just didn't really know your capabilities. Maybe you tried a low percentage shot where the reward wasn't worth the risk.

- Incorrect decisions (e.g., wrong club, wrong target, wrong distance, wrong line of putt, etc.). These might have been perfect shots, but they went to the wrong place. If you had the chance to play the shot again, you would make a different choice.

- Lack of focus (e.g., you forgot to use your pre-shot routine, you didn't concentrate, you allowed external circumstances such as slow play, other players, or the weather bother you, you lost emotional control, etc.). These could occur with any shot, from drives to putts.

- Lack of confidence (e.g., you made the correct club and shot decision, but just weren't really sure you could pull it off, so you didn't fully commit to the shot, etc.).

- Bad swing (e.g., you had all of the above factors under control, but you simply made a bad swing and hit a poor shot). As you think about your round, you may be tempted to attribute lost strokes to "bad swings." Yes, bad swings happen, but try to determine whether one of the above factors really caused the bad swing. For highly skilled golfers, few shots are the result of bad swings in isolation from the above factors.

The following example Golf MasterMind Gap Analysis Worksheet is a chart you can use to analyze your scores. A blank worksheet can be found in Appendix 1 and in the Golf MasterMind Workbook. Use this worksheet on your next few rounds and see if you see any patterns in your gap reasons.

GOLF MASTERMIND GAP ANALYSIS WORKSHEET

		Actual Score	74	78	72	75	77
Strategic Error		Tried low percentage shot				2	1
		Unfamiliar with golf course		2			
		Went for green; didn't lay up					
		Went for pin instead of middle	1				
		Other					
Poor Decision		Wrong club	2				1
		Wrong target		1			
		Wrong line					
		Wrong option on rules situation					
		Other					
Lack of Focus		Forgot to use preshot routine					1
		Bothered by slow play	1			1	
		Bothered by another person					
		External factor (e.g., weather)					
		Lost emotional control		2	1	1	2
		Other					
Lack of Confidence		Wasn't sure of club					
		Had doubts about strategy		1			
		Didn't commit to shot					1
		Didn't take my time					
		Other					
Bad Swing		Miss right			2		
		Miss left		1			1
		Poor Contact (short or long)					
		Total Gap	4	7	3	4	7
		Potential Score	70	71	69	71	70

How to Use the Golf MasterMind Gap Analysis Worksheet

Follow the example shown in the first score column of the chart. A blank Golf MasterMind Gap Analysis Worksheet is included in Appendix 1.

- Enter the date of your round

- Enter your actual score for the round

- Think carefully and realistically about your round and the strokes lost. These could be missed fairways, missed greens, poor approach shots, penalty shots, missed putts, etc. Your goal is to count strokes lost due to errors in strategy, decision-making, loss of focus, or lack of confidence. In other words, you are seeking to identify strokes you could have saved if you had done something different, such as used a different club, tried a different shot, chosen a different target, used your pre-shot routine, backed off when bothered by something, or otherwise changed your approach. For completeness, the Golf MasterMind Gap Analysis worksheet also includes a place to count "bad swings." These are simply strokes lost due to mis-hits that you feel are uncharacteristic for you. You will always have a few bad swings, and sometimes they don't cost you a stroke. As you think about your round, record the bad swings here that do cost you one or more strokes that cannot be accounted for by the above factors.

- Enter your estimate of the number of lost strokes in the corresponding box attributed to each reason. This is a judgment call that you will make based on your reflection on the situation and what happened. For example, you were indecisive about your club selection, and chose the longer club. However, you weren't committed to the choice, and made a poor swing. The ball went into the hazard, costing a total of 2 strokes that could have been saved had you chosen the right club or committed to your decision. If there are multiple reasons for a lost stroke, make your best decision about which one to record on the worksheet.

Try to differentiate between poor shots due to poor swing mechanics or your usual error percentage and those caused by other factors that are within your control, such as those listed above. The key point here is to think about whether, if you could attempt the shot again, you would do something different that could change the outcome. If so, it is an inner game factor. If not, it probably is due to your physical outer game skills, and should be counted as a "bad swing."

- Total the lost strokes; this total is your gap.

- Enter your potential score as your actual score minus your gap.

The purpose of this analysis is to see where you are losing strokes and why it is happening. After you have recorded your gap information for several rounds, you will also be able to see if there are patterns in your gap and where you tend to lose strokes. When you think of your round this way, you will quickly begin to see how you can make dramatic improvement and close the gap between your actual scores and your potential. And, you will also see where your game can be improved by improving your outer game ball-striking skills.

Your Physical Golf Skills – the Outer Game

Your physical golf skills and abilities comprise what I consider to be your "outer game." They include the facets of your game that others can see, including your ball-striking ability, swing speed, ball control, accuracy, short game finesse, and all of the other areas you practice and take lessons to improve. Whether you are a touring professional, a scratch golfer, a weekend player, or a beginner, your outer game ability determines how low your scores can potentially go.

If you are motivated to lower your scores, you will work hard on your outer game, trying to improve your swing mechanics, your short game, and your putting. As your outer game gets better, your potential score will go down, but those improvements may come slowly. It is not so easy to make changes in your outer game that will dramatically lower your potential score.

An equally important source of improvement in your scores will come from refining your inner game, as described above. Ironically, your knowledge of your physical outer game may be the most important part of your inner game, because your skill set and your physical capabilities determine how you attack the golf course (your strategy), how you can perform in an environment without distractions (focus), and how you can execute shots under pressure (confidence).

Whether you are a beginner or a scratch golfer, some areas of your game will always be stronger than others. Even the best PGA and LPGA Tour players are always working to improve. If you want to play to the best of your ability, you should too. There are three steps involved in making meaningful improvement in your golf skills:

1. Collect information on your current abilities through a skills evaluation;

2. Analyze your results to identify improvement opportunities; and

3. Practice with a purpose.

Let's look at each of these steps in more detail.

Evaluate Your Current Skills

The first step to improving your golf skills is to find out where you are right now. But how do you know where you are and where your improvement opportunities lie? To paraphrase the great physicist Lord Kelvin, "you can't improve what you can't measure," and it is true. You need a way to measure your current skill level so that you can determine which skills need the most improvement. And, in order to measure your skills, you need information. That information comes from a skills evaluation.

You already have some knowledge of your golf skills and abilities. However, you may not have detailed information about your game and where your greatest opportunities for improvement lie. There are many ways to assess your strengths and weaknesses, and your PGA or LPGA pro may have a series of skills tests you can take. You can also keep detailed statistics of your rounds to discover your strengths.

Whichever way you evaluate your skills, remember it must serve two purposes:

- To help you better understand your outer game and where you should focus your attention as you practice; and

- To help feed your inner game and give you a detailed and realistic understanding of your true abilities. Your skills evaluation must enable you to quantify your skills in a way that provides realistic data that you can feed into your golf strategy.

The Golf MasterMind Skills Evaluation Worksheet that follows is fairly simplistic and easy to do, yet is comprehensive enough to cover all of the important scoring areas: short putts, long putts, chipping, pitching, bunkers, approach shots, and carry distances. This worksheet provides detailed data that can be used to develop a comprehensive improvement plan for those who want to make a significant improvement in their skills.

Done properly, a skills evaluation will provide a measurement of the status of your game at a point in time. Repeated evaluations taken over time will show trends in your skills – hopefully becoming better and better!

Identify Improvement Opportunities

The second step on the road to improvement is to decide where you want to go, hopefully using your dreams, goals, and objectives from the prior exercises in the chapter on motivation. Once you have the information from the skills evaluations, you can analyze it and truly understand your current strengths and weaknesses.

The goal of your skills analysis should be to identify the highest priority improvement opportunities that will have the biggest impact on lowering your scores. Sometimes these areas will be obvious; other times it may be difficult to decide where you can get the biggest bang for the buck. In either case, you should work with your PGA/LPGA teaching professional to study your skills evaluation information and agree on which areas will be the focus of your improvement practice plan in the next step.

Practice with a Purpose

The final step on the road to improvement is to develop a plan to reach your goals. Once your highest priority improvement opportunities are identified, your PGA/LPGA professional can help you develop a productive practice plan that will focus on your skills improvement priorities.

As you develop your plan to practice with a purpose, consider how much time you spend practicing each area of your game as well as what you do when practicing those areas. Many times what is needed is not simply more hours of practice, but rather a different allocation of your practice time so that you are spending the right amount of time on the right areas of your game.

For example, most golfers love to hit drivers and full shots on the range. This is not a bad thing, as these are important shots in every round of golf. However, many people will spend 50% or more of their practice time hitting drivers and full shots, when in fact those shots account for only around 25% of strokes taken in an average round. On the other hand, short game shots around the green, including putting, account for nearly 60% of strokes taken. These critical scoring areas frequently receive only a small fraction of practice time.

The simple act of doing these evaluations and collecting the information will help you learn many things about your own golf game. Then as you repeat the evaluations and update your results after practice, you will be able to see your improvement in the numbers and your scores.

Once you identify areas that need improvement, Appendix 2 contains suggestions for practice games that you can play – either alone or with a friend – to sharpen your skills. I am a strong proponent of using skill-based games to help make your practice time more enjoyable and purposeful. These games will help you focus on each specific skill measured in the evaluation process.

Golf MasterMind Skills Evaluation Worksheet

Skill	Date	1	2	3	4	5	6	7	8	9	10	TOTAL	STANDARD
Short Putt 4 ft (max 5)													1
Long Putt 30 ft (max 10)													20
Short Chip 45 ft (max 20)													30
Long Chip 60 ft (max 20)													35
Pitch 20-25 yds (max 20)													40
Greenside Bunker (max 20)													40
Approach 40 yds (max 40)													100
Approach 60 yds (max 40)													150
Approach 80 yds (max 40)													150
Approach 100 yds (max 40)													150

How to Use the Golf MasterMind Skills Evaluation Worksheet

The Golf MasterMind Skills Evaluation Worksheet is simple to use and can quickly help you assess your physical outer game strengths and opportunities for improvement. Each skill evaluation area involves hitting 10 balls as described below. After each ball comes to rest, record the distance in feet the ball lies from the hole, always rounding up to the next number of feet.

For example, any miss is at least "1." If you miss by 1½ feet, write down "2", and so on. You don't need to use a tape measurer; it is okay to estimate the distances as long as you are consistent. Notice that each skill has a maximum miss value, so if you miss by more than the maximum, simply write in the maximum for that ball. It can also be helpful to note whether your misses are due to distance control or aiming issues.

Total your results from all 10 trials for each skill and compare to the standard. When you discover a skill that needs improvement, refer to the practice games suggested below; these games are included in Appendix 2. Following are detailed instructions and references to corresponding practice games for each area of the Golf MasterMind Skills Evaluation Worksheet.

Short and Long Putt Skills Evaluations

Find two locations on the putting green where you can putt from 4 feet and 30 feet to the hole. As described above, record the distance that each putt finishes from the hole. For short putts, use a maximum of 5 feet for any ball. For long putts, use a maximum of 10 feet for any ball. The first few times you do these evaluations, keep things simple and start all putts along the same line, with little if any break. As you improve, you can repeat the evaluation with different slopes and angles to make it more challenging.

Suggested short putt practice games:
- Clockwork
- Line It Up

- School
- Sequence
- Wicket Trail

Suggested long putt practice games:
- Batter Up!
- Catch Me If You Can
- LagMaster
- Line It Up
- School
- Sequence
- Sneak Attack
- Wicket Trail

Chipping Skills Evaluations

Find a place on fringe of the putting green where you will have a good lie and can chip from 45 feet and 60 feet to different holes. All chips should be across a flat green with little or no break. Record the distance that each chip finishes from the hole. Use a maximum of 20 feet for any ball. If you find that you are consistently beating the standard, make your chipping trials more difficult by varying the slope and type of lie (e.g. from the rough, into the grain, etc.).

Suggested chipping practice games:
- Air Mail
- Batter Up!
- Catch Me If You Can
- Club Tricks
- Landing Zone
- Sequence
- Sneak Attack

Pitching Skills Evaluation

Find a place 15 yards from the edge of the putting green where you will have a good lie and can pitch approximately 25-30 yards to the hole. There should be around 10-15 yards from the edge of the green to the hole, in addition to the 15 yards from the pitching location to the edge of the green. Select a location where the ball can land and roll across a flat green with little or no break.

Record the distance that each pitch finishes from the hole. Use a maximum of 20 feet for any ball. If you find that you are consistently beating the standard, make your pitching trials more difficult by varying the type of lie (e.g., from the rough) and the challenge of the shot (e.g., over a bunker, uphill, downhill, etc.).

Suggested pitching practice games:
- Air Mail
- Batter Up!
- Catch Me (If You Can)
- Club Tricks
- Landing Zone
- Sequence
- Sneak Attack

Bunker Skills Evaluation

Find a place in a greenside bunker where you will have a good lie about 10-15 yards from the hole. The shot should be across a flat green with little or no break. Record the distance that each bunker shot finishes from the hole. Use a maximum of 20 feet for any ball. If you find that you are consistently beating the standard, make your bunker trials more difficult by varying the type of lie (e.g., soft and hard sand, buried lies, etc.) and the challenge of the shot (e.g., uphill, downhill, etc.).

Suggested bunker practice games:
- Air Mail

- Batter Up!
- Catch Me If You Can
- Club Tricks
- Landing Zone
- Sequence
- Sneak Attack

Approach Shot Skills Evaluation

Find a place where you can hit approach shots to a practice green. If this is not possible, you may use the driving range if you will be able to measure how far away your shots will come to rest from a target. Use a laser range finder and measure points at 40, 60, 80, and 100 yards from the hole or your range target. It is best to do this assessment with a partner who can measure and record each shot after you hit it.

Record the distance that each shot finishes from the hole. Use a maximum of 40 feet for any ball. If you find that you are consistently beating the standard, make your approach trials more difficult by varying the type of lie (e.g., from the rough) and the challenge of the shot (e.g., over a bunker, uphill, downhill, etc.).

Suggested approach shot practice games:
- Air Mail
- Catch Me If You Can
- Club Tricks
- Sequence
- Sneak Attack

Golf MasterMind Skills Evaluation Summary

Remember, you are looking for patterns in your skills that can help you isolate your most important opportunities for improvement. You are also looking for where your results are inconsistent. Inconsistent results can help you identify a swing mechanics or technique issue that can be addressed with your PGA or LPGA teaching professional. Your consistency equates to your probability of success when you attempt a shot on the golf course. This information will be important in the following chapter on strategy.

Carry Distances Evaluation

Every golfer needs to know the exact yardage his or her ball carries with each club. The following Golf MasterMind Carry Distance Evaluation Worksheet provides a way for you to record your carry distances with your clubs so you can develop a yardage chart for your entire set.

Golf MasterMind Carry Distance Evaluation Worksheet

Club	Date	1	2	3	4	5	6	7	8	9	10	Average	Middle 4 Expected	Consistency Factor
EXAMPLE	9/7	145	137	128	142	133	137	141	127	140	138	137	138	6
Driver														
3-Wood														
5-Wood														
4-iron or hybrid														
5-iron														
6-iron														
7-iron														
8-iron														
9-iron														
Pitching Wedge														
Gap Wedge														
Sand Wedge														

How to Use the Golf MasterMind Carry Distance Evaluation Worksheet

Use each club from a good lie in the fairway or on the driving range and watch where each shot lands (not where it comes to rest). Measure the distance with a laser range finder. It is best to do this assessment with a partner who can measure and record the actual carry yardage for each shot after you hit. If you are fortunate enough to have access to a radar launch monitor device, you can use the yardages estimated by that system. Record the yardages on the worksheet as shown in the example. Make sure you record 10 results for each club.

Now it is time for a bit of math. This can seem a bit tricky, but it is actually fairly simple, and the results can be extremely helpful. Refer to the "example" line of the worksheet to see what the numbers will look like. Try doing the calculations on the example to ensure you can follow the procedure. If all else fails, go to www.golfermastermindpro.com and you can download the Golf MasterMind app to do the calculations for you. Here is how to do it:

1. Calculate your "Average" distance by adding up the distances for each shot and then dividing by the number of shots you recorded (you should have measured 10 shots). The total of the example distances is 1,368, which gives an average of 136.8. Then, round this number to the nearest yard, giving you an average carry distance of 137 yards for this club.

2. Calculate your "Middle 4 Expected" carry distance. I consider this to be a better number to use than your average when you are making club selections, because it ignores your best and worst shots. As shown in the example, highlight your three shortest and three longest distances. Then average the remaining four numbers. Add them up and divide the total by four. In this example, the total is 552, so the "middle 4 expected" carry distance is 138 yards (552/4). Round this number to the nearest yard.

3. Finally (this is where things get really interesting), calculate your "Consistency Factor." If you know something about statistics, you will recognize this as the "standard deviation." If not, no problem. – just follow along. This is an important number because it shows how many yards either less than or more than your average carry distance you can expect most of your shots to fly. To calculate your consistency factor, follow these steps:

   a. Take each of the 10 distances one at a time and subtract your average carry distance. For example, the first number is 145, which gives us 145-137=8. Square this number: 8X8=64 and either write it down or add it in your calculator's memory.

   b. Repeat this calculation for each of the remaining carry yardages.

   c. Then add all ten of these numbers (you should get 312) and average them (divide the total by 10). You should have 31.2.

   d. Finally, calculate the square root of this result (you should get 5.59). Round this number _up_ to the next whole number, giving you 6 yards. That number is your standard deviation, which is the difference in yards from your average carry distance you should expect to see for that club.

This means that you would expect to be able to carry the ball with this club 137 yards (your real average), but don't be surprised if it only goes 131 yards. Your best shots with that club might fly 143 yards, but most will fall somewhere between 131 and 143 yards, with the average being 137 yards.

Pay close attention to your results, especially to variations in carry distance. If your consistency factor is a large number, your distances with that club are less predictable. You may need to work on your swing or modify your practice routine to gain consistency. You want to be able to hit each club with consistent, predictable carry yardages to help you make the proper club selection on the course. If you have wide variations due to poor shots, think about those poor shots and their causes. Use face impact tape to determine whether you are consistently hitting the ball on the "sweet spot." Do you tend to hit these shots "thin" (not brushing the grass) or "fat" (hitting the grass behind the ball)?

In reviewing the Golf MasterMind Skills Evaluation Worksheet, if you find an area that seems to need improvement, you should seek help from your PGA or LPGA professional and develop or modify your practice routine to focus more time on that area. Review the suggested practice games and incorporate one or more of them into your practice sessions.

When you have completed these skills evaluations, you should look back to the prior section on your inner game and reflect on your gap analysis and your Golf MasterMind survey. Remember, your focus here is on both lowering your potential score through skills improvement and on reducing your gap so you can play up to your potential.

Much of your opportunity to improve your scores comes from knowing what your realistically can and cannot do and playing to your strengths. Further opportunities to improve lie in improving your physical skills. These skills evaluations should help you take advantage of both.

•   •   •

The second level of the Peak Performance Pyramid is ability, which refers to your ability to manage your inner game to take maximum advantage of your physical outer game. We all want to improve our scores, and the Golf MasterMind concept views your opportunities to improve in two ways.

First and most familiar is improvement in your outer game, which includes ball-striking, swing mechanics, short game, and all of the parts of your game that others can observe. Improvement in these areas will lower your potential score, but these improvements don't happen overnight. And, although improving your skills can lower your potential score, this will not automatically lower your actual score. In fact, this can merely increase your gap unless you also work to sharpen your inner game.

Second is improvement in your inner game, which includes your knowledge of your outer game abilities and your ability to manage yourself to capitalize on your physical skills. Improvements in your inner game *can* happen overnight, and they begin by knowing your abilities and playing to your strengths. The following chapters will show you how.

CHAPTER THREE

"Strategy is thinking about a choice and choosing to stick with your thinking."

- Anon.

Strategy

The third level of the Peak Performance Pyramid is Strategy. This level deals with how you use your physical outer skills and inner mental game to your advantage as you battle against "old man par." It is easy to understand the importance of strategy with games such as chess, cards, Clash of Clans, and Candy Crush, among many others.

In any game, there is a best way to move your piece, play your card, attack with your troops, or match objects. When you make the correct move, you are rewarded. When you make a poor choice of moves, you feel the consequences of your choice.

The same is true of golf. However, for a variety of reasons, I think that many golfers don't sense the importance of strategy in playing golf. One reason is that even if you do have a strategy, it may be difficult to follow as planned due to the wide range of possible outcomes for each shot. In other words, your skill level might not support your strategy.

For example, you might intend to aim down the left side of the fairway to set up a better angle of approach to the green. However, your ball-striking skills are not reliable enough to hit that shot consistently. Instead of going down the left side, your ball ends up in the right rough. You might begin to think that it doesn't matter where you aim, or that it is just luck if it ends up where you intended it to go, so why bother strategizing? This phenomenon doesn't exist in most games.

The chess analogy for this would be where you intended to move your bishop to a certain square, but it mysteriously ended up on a different square. If this happened often, you certainly would lose interest in strategizing your moves. Why bother developing a strategy for a series of moves if you are unable to move your piece to the desired square? And, you might be interested in taking chess-piece moving lessons!

My point is this: in most games, you have the capability to execute your strategy perfectly. You may or may not have the best strategy, but you will be able to carry it out as planned. If you plan to move your pawn forward one square, you will be able to do it to perfection. Golf is different, in that your success in implementing any strategy is highly dependent upon your level of skill. You may plan to hit over the hazard, but you might not succeed.

Another reason is that the consequences of a poor strategy are not always immediately apparent. You might strategize to cut the corner on a dogleg and then hit the perfect tee shot as planned, right around the corner. You didn't know it from the tee box, but this strategy was flawed because your next shot is much more difficult from that position than it would have been if you had played a more conservative tee shot. This could then cascade into more trouble with subsequent shots. Because the end result (your double-bogey) is far removed from the seemingly perfect tee shot you hit 15 minutes before, you might not attribute the difficulties to your poor choice of strategy off the tee. You might blame the outcome on a poor chip or a bad putt. Certainly, those shots might have contributed to the problem, but perhaps those aspects of your game were stressed from the difficulty presented by where your tee shot landed.

Staying with the chess analogy, the example would be where you chose a poor strategy and made the move you wanted to make. Your move then set in motion a series of moves from your opponent who, delighted that you played right into her trap, checkmates you. You might not realize which move led to your demise, and might not attribute it to your poor strategy many moves prior.

So, in golf, it could be strategy or execution that is responsible for the outcome on any hole. Unfortunately, you cannot do much in the short term about your ability to execute your intended shot. You are stuck with your physical outer game, your skill set, and your level of consistency, at least until you spend serious effort on your swing mechanics. You can, however, improve your strategy, and it does matter.

When you prepare to hit your ball, you have to envision where you want your ball to go. You have to select a club. When you address your ball, you have to aim somewhere. You have to try to hit a certain shot. A Golf MasterMind makes the best possible choices on each shot, and accepts the outcome if it doesn't come off exactly as planned.

A Moving Target

Just as with other games such as chess, your strategy for playing a hole is a moving target, shifting and adjusting as needed to deal with where your ball lies in relation to the hole. For example, standing on the tee, you see a short, easy par 4 that you feel is a birdie hole. There are some bunkers in front of the green and water behind, but they need not factor into your thinking at this point. Your strategy is to hit an iron to the wide part of the fairway, leaving a wedge to the green for your best chance to make a birdie. All good so far.

However, you mis-hit the iron and your ball lands in thick rough to the right of the fairway, leaving a difficult shot over deep bunkers to a shallow green with a water hazard right behind the green. Now, the hole doesn't look quite as easy as it did from the tee. If only you had ended up in the fairway as you had intended, you might still think of it as a birdie hole. Now, from this position, a par 4 would be a great score, and you might be happy with a bogey 5. Should you change your strategy or continue trying to hit your second shot close to the hole to give yourself a birdie chance?

In this simple example, it may seem obvious that you should adjust your strategy to deal with the challenges that you face. In fact, a Golf MasterMind will adjust his or her strategy before *every* shot, always seeking the easiest way to make the lowest expected score from wherever the ball lies, without regard to what led to the current position of the ball. At this point, the original strategy is irrelevant and must be replaced by an updated or new strategy.

As with any game, your strategy for the moment is dependent on your situation and the various factors that could influence how you might play your next shot. The following section explores these factors in detail.

Factors Influencing Your Strategy

It should be clear that you need a strategy for each shot you hit. Standing on the tee, you have a strategy for how you can best play the hole. Once you have hit that shot, you have a revised strategy for how to play the hole from where your ball lies. Along the way, many factors will act to influence your strategy. As a Golf MasterMind, you should consider each of these as you plan your attack on par. Some of these are:

1. Your Abilities

    Chapter 2 discussed your physical "outer game" skills and your mental "inner game" abilities. In order for you to develop a successful strategy for a shot, you must know your capabilities. This means you must know not only what you are capable of doing, but also your probability of actually being able to do it.

    For example, you might be able to hit a 8-iron 140 yards in the air. However, when you did the "Carry Distance" skills evaluation, your actual carry yardage on ten trials ranged from 127 yards to 145 yards, with six of the ten shots (60%) carrying less than 140 yards and your consistency factor with that club is 6 yards. Yes, you are *able* to carry an 8-iron 140 yards, but it isn't likely to happen, especially under the stress of having to carry a water hazard or deep greenside bunker.

    As another example, if your ball is on the fringe, you may be tempted to chip to the hole. Your "Chipping" skills evaluation shows that your average chip from 45 feet stops 12 feet from the hole. However, your average long putt stops 5 feet from the hole. Perhaps it would be better to putt from off the green.

My point is that you must have accurate, detailed, realistic knowledge of your skills and abilities in order to develop a viable strategy for any shot. This is no time for showing off, and there is no place for ego. You must know what you can expect to do with every club, and be able to adjust your expectations to deal with a variety of situations. Yes, you can fly a ball 140 yards with your 8-iron, but can you count on it? What about if your ball is in the rough? How does that change your abilities?

Once you have this knowledge, you can make good decisions on how to play a shot, without requiring that you hit a perfect 8-iron that you are only capable of doing some 40% of the time.

The purpose of this knowledge is to allow you to play to your strengths. Your strategy should, where possible, allow you to play the shot that gives you the greatest chance of success, allowing for your expected ability under the conditions with which you are faced.

2.   Your Intention

Your strategy for any shot should be influenced by your intention; that is what you are trying to do. Are you intending to be aggressive? Are you playing safe? These questions could have different answers from shot to shot and hole to hole.

For every skill level and in every circumstance, there is a "best" way to play a shot. It should be your intention to identify this way, which is unique for you and your game. If you are playing match play, you might choose to be aggressive. If you are coming up the 18th hole trying to make a par for your career best score, you might be more conservative.

3.   The Risk-Reward Equation

The question of intention leads to the question of risk vs. reward. As you consider your strategy for a shot, you must consider the possible outcomes of each option. As with stock market investments, business decisions, and most games, the risk you take must be accompanied by a commensurate reward.

With each shot, you have some level of risk that you will make a mistake that will lead to a higher score. However, taking that risk also gives you the opportunity for a lower score if you are successful. The risk-reward equation is about evaluating the risks and the potential rewards to help you select the best shot strategy. The goal is for you to always choose the shot strategy that will produce the minimum expected score.

Expected score means the average score you would make if you attempted the shot multiple times. You may never actually shoot the expected score, because an expected score frequently is a number like "3.6," "4.5," or "6.2." These numbers are the result of a mathematical calculation that combines the best case and worst case scenarios of a shot strategy with your estimate of the probability of those scenarios occurring. In order to fully explain the risk-reward equation, things have to get a bit technical. However, your actual risk-reward decisions on the golf course will probably be made more by instinct. Behind that instinct, though, some serious math and statistics calculations are going on, and I think it is important to understand how it works.

The risk-reward equation goes like this:

$$Expected\ Score = \quad P(success) * (score\ if\ successful) +$$
$$\left(1 - P(success)\right) * (score\ if\ unsuccessful)$$

This may look like fancy math, but it is really quite simple, and a Golf MasterMind subconsciously does a "gut feel" version of it in his or her head on every shot. The equation says that your expected score equals the probability that you will succeed with your attempted shot, multiplied by the score you are likely to make if you succeed, plus the probability that you will fail at your attempted shot, multiplied by the score you are likely to make if you fail.

A simple example works like this: you have a 50/50 chance of hitting the green. Therefore, you have a 50% probability of hitting the green, and if you succeed, you will make a par 4. You also have a 50% probability of missing the green. If you miss the green you will make a bogey 5. Your expected score is then (.5 * 4) + (.5 * 5), which equals 4.5. Here are more examples:

Let's say that your ball is in thick rough, and you have that same 150 yard shot to the green over a water hazard that I discussed above. Just to the right of the green is a paved cart path, and just beyond the path is out of bounds. Directly over the green is a thick group of shrubs and bushes. The reward for hitting the green is a chance at birdie. The risk is a chance at disaster. You feel your probability of hitting the green from this situation is about 10%. What should you do?

Your ego says "go for it." Your scorecard says double-bogey.

In reality, you should make an unemotional, unbiased assessment of the situation and do the math. Let's stay with this scenario, where you have a 10% chance of hitting the green. If you do hit the green, you have a 20% chance of making the birdie putt and an 80% chance of 2-putting for par (let's not even talk about your chances of 3-putting for bogey!). This gives you an expected score of 3.8 if you hit the green: (.2 x 3) + (.8 x 4) = 3.8.

If you miss the green, you will be lucky to make a double-bogey. You might end up in the hazard, hitting your fourth shot from the drop zone (still having to carry the hazard). Or, you might go out of bounds, requiring that you drop back in the thick rough and reconsider your strategy. Or, you might go over the green into an unplayable lie or difficult situation in the bushes and shrubs. Each of these could lead to making a double- or triple-bogey, or worse. There is probably no need to even do the math on this scenario. Let's just say that missing the green gives you an expected score of 6.5.

Doing the risk-reward calculation, a choice to go for the green has a 10% chance of a reward score of 3.8 if you are successful. This must be balanced against the risk of hitting into the hazard, out of bounds, or unplayable lie, which has 90% chance of an expected score of double-bogey 6 or higher. The meager reward of this strategy is far outweighed by the risk of disaster. Your expected score if going for the green would be (.1 x 3.8) + (.9 x 6.5) = 6.2. Therefore, going for the green will most likely lead to double-bogey or worse.

On the other hand, a choice to chip out to the fairway will leave you with an easy wedge to the green. This choice has an expected score of 4.8: on the green in three plus a 20% chance of a 1-putt for par and an 80% chance of a 2-putt for bogey. This choice sacrifices the chance at a birdie, but essentially eliminates the chance of a disaster. You may not like the idea of playing for bogey, but sometimes that is the safe play.

A simpler way to look at the risk-reward equation can be shown in the following tables. These tables show the expected scores for likely combinations of best-case / worst-case scenarios:

If you feel you have a 0% chance of succeeding with the shot:

Golf MasterMind Expected Score Table			
Best Case Score	**Worst Case Score**		
	4	5	6	7
2	You don't *really* need a data table to help you decide <u>not</u> to try this shot, do you?		
3			
4			
5			

I know this first table seems silly, but sometimes we do think about trying the "impossible" shot, in hopes of some miracle or incredible luck. This is fun in practice, and I encourage you to try these shots from under bushes, behind trees, over water from deep grass, or wherever there is virtually no realistic chance of pulling it off. Try them to discover what you can really do with your golf ball from crazy situations. Try them to understand your limits. Try them to find out how bad things can go when you make poor decisions. But don't try them when it matters!

If you feel you have a 1/3 chance of succeeding with the shot:

Golf MasterMind Expected Score Table				
Best Case Score	**Worst Case Score**			
	4	**5**	**6**	**7**
2	3.3	4	5.3	6.3
3		4.3	5	5.7
4			5.3	6
5				6.3

This table shows your expected scores where you have a slim (33%) chance of success. These are worth trying as long as the worst case scenario isn't too bad. I am not even showing the expected scores where your worst case score is only one stroke higher than your best case score. There is so little risk in these situations that there is no need to worry. Go ahead and try these shots! I have highlighted the boxes where your expected score is two strokes or more higher than your best case score. It probably isn't worth trying those shots.

You feel you have a 50/50 chance of succeeding with the shot:

Golf MasterMind Expected Score Table				
Best Case Score	**Worst Case Score**			
	4	**5**	**6**	**7**
2	3	3.5	4	4.5
3		4	4.5	5
4			5	5.5
5				6

This table shows your expected scores where you have a fair (50%) chance of success. Like the prior scenario, these are worth trying as long as the worst case scenario isn't too bad. I have highlighted the boxes where your expected score is two strokes or more higher than your best case score. It probably isn't worth trying these shots.

You feel you have a 2/3 chance of succeeding with the shot:

Golf MasterMind Expected Score Table				
Best Case Score	**Worst Case Score**			
	4	**5**	**6**	**7**
2	2.7	3	3.3	3.7
3		3.7	4	4.3
4			4.7	5
5				5.7

This table shows your expected scores where you have a high (67%) chance of success. These are worth trying if you can accept the worst case score, since your expected score is not too much worse than your best case score.

An even simpler way to look at the risk-reward equation is to just think about the positives and negatives of your situation. If all of this math and these tables seem too complex or cumbersome for you, don't worry. No one really does this math in their head on the golf course.

However, a Golf MasterMind will think like this: if I succeed with my intended shot, what score am I likely to make? If I don't succeed, what score am I likely to make? What is the best thing that could happen? What is the worst? If I had ten tries to hit this shot, how many would be successful? In the above scenario, going for the green gives you a slight chance at birdie with a high probability of disaster. Playing safe gives you a high probability of bogey with a slight chance of disaster.

If you are honest with your assessment of the situation, you will know which shot to hit. Or, if you are 100% comfortable with the risk and the higher score that will come with a miss, then you will have an easy decision.

This is perhaps an extreme example, but I was caddying for a player (my son) recently who had the exact scenario that I described above with the hazard, the cart path, and the deep rough. I'll leave it to your imagination to decide what choice he made. I will say that (I hope) a lesson was learned about balancing risk with reward.

Certainly, there are many situations that will favor taking the risk. For example, if the drop zone in the above scenario was on the green side of the hazard and no out of bounds or bushes were near the green, the risk would diminish greatly, and the best strategy could be to go for the green. Every situation is different, and each shot requires that you consider both the positive and negative possibilities before you commit to a strategy.

Here is another example. Suppose you are on a par 5, with a chance to reach the green in two. Reaching the green would give you a putt for eagle, and a likely birdie. Your expected score would be 4. However, it is a long shot to reach the green, and you would have to hit your driver "off the deck" to get there. We all know how risky it can be hitting a driver from the fairway. But, what if there are no water hazards or out of bounds threats, and only a few greenside bunkers lie between you and the green?

Your other option is to lay up to 100 yards using a 6-iron. Laying up leaves you a chance at birdie, with an almost certain par. What would a Golf MasterMind do in this situation?

I think he or she would hit the driver, and here is why. A perfectly struck driver from the fairway could reach the green, or perhaps end up in one of the greenside bunkers. The bunkers pose no major threat, leaving a good chance to get on the green with a short birdie putt. That's the reward. The worst thing that could happen with the driver is to top it or otherwise miss-hit the shot, which probably would end up rolling the ball to right about where the 6-iron layup shot would go. That's the risk… and it isn't much of a risk. In this case, the difference between the risk (worst case score) and the reward (best case score) is quite small, so it is an easy decision to use the driver (assuming you have practiced that shot a few times!).

To recap the risk-reward analysis, A Golf MasterMind will always consider the best, worst, and likely outcomes for any given choice of club or shot. The final decision comes down to making sure the potential reward is worth the risk.

I'll finish the risk-reward discussion with one more example. I was caddying for my son in an important tournament, and we knew he had a 2-stroke lead with two holes to play. The 17th hole was a par 5, reachable in two shots, but the green was fronted by a pond. Any shot to the green would have to carry the water by at least 5 yards, or it would roll back down the slope and find a watery grave. He could reach the green with a good 4-hybrid or lay up with a short iron, and so we had the risk-reward discussion.

He didn't need to make a birdie; he only needed to par the last two holes. Our discussion went something like this: Me: "Going for the green right now won't win the tournament for you, but it might just lose it." Him: "Give me the 8-iron."

As Roy McAvoy's caddy said in "Tin Cup," "Sometimes par is good enough to win."

That is how a Golf MasterMind thinks.

4.   External Factors

Your strategy for playing any shot must also account for factors that are beyond your control. These external factors include wind, rain, temperature, spectators, slow play, the lie of your ball, and even such things as temporary immovable obstructions if you are lucky or skilled enough to be playing in an event with grandstands.

In chapter 2, you developed a carry yardage chart, hopefully for every club in your bag. You probably measured your yardages in good, if not ideal conditions on the range. However, it gets windy on the golf course, and your ball ends up in thick grass, thin grass, sandy areas, and on slopes. You must be able to adjust your expected abilities for an almost infinite range of conditions. It could take a long time to fill out your yardage chart to account for that many scenarios!

Still, you need to know how these varying conditions will affect your playing abilities, and thus your strategy for each shot. Skilled golfers make these adjustments almost subconsciously, based on feel. They also change how they hit the ball to counteract the effects of wind. You may or may not have the ball-striking skills to make these adjustments. If not, your playing strategy will have to adapt by changing clubs as needed.

Regardless of which method you choose, a Golf MasterMind knows that it is not nice to fight Mother Nature. If it is windy take more club and swing slower. If your ball lies in a divot, take more club, grip down, and play a safe angle. If you are in thick rough, take your medicine and get back to the short stuff. As discussed above, your strategy is an ever-changing, fluid moving target that must account for factors beyond your control.

5. Your Level of Confidence

Lastly, your strategy for the golf course, a hole, and any shot should be influenced by your level of confidence. If, after accounting for any and all of the above factors, you are unsure about your strategy for the shot, you are not likely to succeed. There is almost nothing worse than addressing the ball and swinging with doubts about what you are attempting to do.

I can think of many times where I have been in this situation, and forged ahead anyway with my swing, doubting but hoping for the best. I can say with great authority that hope is not the best ball-striker.

Chapter 5 discusses the element of confidence in greater detail. For now, however, remember that you must believe in your ability to carry out your intended strategy.

Sticking With It

The final element of strategy is to follow it. What I mean is that once you have a plan of attack for a hole and a strategy for each shot, you should stick with *your* strategy. I have emphasized "your" because it is so easy for us to be influenced by others. Another "war" story:

I was caddying for my son in a state championship, and he was tied for the lead after shooting 1-under par in the first round. The first hole was a dogleg right par 5, curving around a water hazard. There was a huge oak tree right at the corner of the dogleg, much too big to go over. We had practiced the hole by playing around the tree, and he had birdied the hole in the first round by following that strategy.

Then came the second round, playing with the co-leader who was a much longer hitter. That boy stepped up to the tee and easily smashed his ball over the water and close to the green.

My son teed his ball and set up to try the same shot.

Before even hitting his first shot in the final round of an important tournament, he was ready to abandon his proven successful strategy for playing that hole. Why? Because he felt he needed to keep up with his competitor. I won't tell what ensued, but I will say that it wasn't pretty.

This issue may seem to present a paradox. I have said that your strategy for playing any shot is an "ever-changing, fluid moving target," and that it needs to be adjusted to account for the situation that faces you. That is true. However, it usually should not be adjusted in reaction to what another player does (some match play situations may be exceptions to this rule). Just as race horses wear blinkers to keep them focused on what lies ahead, you must ignore both the good and bad things that may be happening around you. As I wrote at the beginning of this chapter, it is you against "old man par." To shoot your best scores, play your own game.

A Golf MasterMind always develops the best strategy for his or her own shot, without regard to what other players may do or think.

•   •   •

One of my students is an elite player. He is highly competitive and motivated to excel. His ball-striking skills are superb, his short game is sharp, and he is a good putter. He generally plays very well in tournaments, and finishes in the top five most of the time. Someone once asked him what made him better than the other players, all of whom have similar ball-striking skills. My student wasn't sure, and didn't really have an answer.

I did.

He is different in two ways. Although he is not yet a Golf MasterMind Pro, he is an excellent strategic thinker. He thinks through all of the possibilities, both good and bad, and usually selects the best strategy to match his abilities to the situation and the circumstances. Also an excellent chess player and gamer, he understands the importance of thinking ahead and playing to his strengths. He knows well what types of shots he can and cannot realistically make. He doesn't worry about trying to keep up with longer hitters.

Second, he has an amazing ability to focus when it is time to play a shot. And that is the topic of the next chapter.

CHAPTER FOUR

"Concentration comes out of a combination of confidence and hunger."

- Arnold Palmer

Focus

And now it is time to focus on the fourth level of the Peak Performance Pyramid, and perhaps the critical element in becoming a Golf MasterMind Pro. Indeed, focus is so important that everything that has come before is worthless without it. Motivation gets you to the practice range and keeps you going in the face of setbacks and challenges. Your ball-striking skills give you the potential to play to your ability. Your strategy shows the way to play your best.

And then, in the moment of truth as you prepare to hit your shot, you could lose it all if you don't pay attention to the business of hitting the ball. But what is "focus?"

I hear others say it all of the time, and I'm probably guilty of saying it too often when I'm caddying: "Come on now, focus on this shot." I even say it to myself when I'm playing. What I mean is that, in golf terms, focus is the point where the critical factors of time management, time travel, uncontrollables, and emotional management come together when it is time to swing. These are four unique challenges that make it surprisingly difficult to focus during a round of golf.

Let's explore each of these to understand them and their potential impact on your golf performance.

1. Time Management

Many sports, like baseball, football, soccer, and basketball are mostly reactive sports. The batter reacts to the pitch. The fielder reacts to the fly ball. The quarterback reacts to the defense and the unfolding pass coverage. The defense reacts to the run or the pass. In sports like these, usually only one person on the team is not reactive, but rather is proactive. The pitcher decides what pitch to throw and where to place it. He or she initiates the action. The field goal kicker blocks out the crowd and envisions the ball flying between the uprights. Alone, the foul shooter tosses the ball through the hoop. Everyone else waits and reacts to the shot.

Golf is proactive like these examples, only more so. Everything that happens to your golf ball is solely up to you. To make things more challenging, only a small part of your time on the golf course is spent actually playing golf.

For example, in the course of a 5-hour round of golf, you will spend about one hour thinking about hitting your ball and preparing to hit the shot. You will spend only about three minutes actually hitting your ball. That leaves three hours and 57 minutes of downtime between shots.

It is impossible for you to remain focused on the business of hitting your golf ball (that one hour and three minute timeframe) for the entire time that you are on the golf course. How should you spend that time?

In Steve Williams' book "Golf at the Top," he relates how one of his most important functions as Tiger Woods' caddie was to talk to Tiger about anything but golf between shots. Competitive golf is intense; relaxation is imperative.

All I can say about that downtime is to enjoy being outdoors with your friends or fellow competitors. Golf courses are some of the most beautiful places in the world. Enjoy this time and, for the most part, *don't* think too much about your round of golf. Especially, don't dwell on whatever has happened to this point in your round. Have fun with your partners, discuss topics of interest, and allow your brain to relax.

This is important, because as you approach your ball, you need to prepare to focus. Like the pitcher, the field goal kicker, and the foul shooter, you must put everything aside and get to work. So, a Golf MasterMind has a tiny "on-off switch" embedded in his or her brain. The switch goes on when it is time to hit the ball, and it goes off once the ball has come to rest.

There are three parts to what I call this "business of hitting your golf ball." These are your pre-shot routine, your in-shot routine, and your post-shot routine. When the switch goes on, here is what happens.

Pre-Shot Routine – Most descriptions of a pre-shot routine begin once your club has been selected and it is time to swing. A Golf MasterMind starts his or her pre-shot routine on arrival at the ball. Most importantly, a Golf MasterMind uses the same pre-shot routine consistently on every shot – that is why it is called a "routine." A great pre-shot routine has three components: think, feel, and act.

- **Think**

    This is where you evaluate your situation, assess the lie of your ball, the conditions and factors that will affect your shot, and consider your options for playing the shot. Thinking requires that you remember your club carry distances and adjust them for the conditions, such as wind or a bad lie. Thinking means that you assess the risks and the possible rewards associated with your shot. Thinking also requires that you develop a strategy for the shot that will capitalize on your ball-striking skills and account for the risk-reward balance that you can accept.

    "Think" means that you consider all of the factors that will affect the shot and make the best club choice, select the best target, and select the best type of shot to play for you to be successful. By "successful," I mean the shot that will give you your lowest expected score from wherever your ball lies to the hole.

- **Feel**

This is where you envision your shot, usually by standing behind the ball and imagining your ball flying to your target exactly the way you would like it to fly. "Feel" means to see your ball as though watching a movie, landing where you want it to go. "Feel" means feeling relaxed and comfortable with the shot you are intending to hit. "Feel" means to think of how you want to feel when the ball comes to rest. "Feel" means to swing your club and rehearse, or feel the type of shot you want to hit. "Feel" means to be confident that you have made the correct choices and that you are free to act.

- **Act**

Finally, this is where you actually address the ball and prepare to swing. "Act" means to step up to the ball, look at your target, and swing.

In-Shot Routine

Your in-shot routine is simple: trust that you have prepared for this moment, and swing. It is over in about one second, but it might take years of lessons to learn.

Post-Shot Routine

You may not have thought much about having a post-shot routine, but I'm sure you do have one. You do something after hitting your ball, but perhaps it isn't what could be called "routine." A Golf MasterMind reverses the pre-shot routine and uses this brief time to end the current shot, turn off the switch, and move on. A great post-shot routine, then, has the same three components as a great pre-shot routine, but in reverse order: act, feel, and think.

Act

This is where you stand there, perfectly balanced and holding your finish in a "tour pose," watching your ball fly. You may do many things during this time, including talking to your ball (research shows they don't listen), waving your club around, etc. However, as a teaching professional, I can assure you that the simple fact of knowing that you must hold a balanced finish and tour pose will actually help you make a better swing.

If you don't believe this, think of the opposite. What are the chances that a terrible swing will lead to a beautifully balanced finish, with you holding your finish like a tour pro? There is something about knowing what you must do at the end of your swing that helps you do some things right during the swing.

So, "act" means to look like a pro, no matter where your ball is going. "Act" means to smooth out the turf or fill your divot. "Act" means to put your club away and prepare to move on.

Feel

This is where you accept your shot. You don't have to like it (I'll discuss this in detail under emotional management), but you must accept it. Whatever it was, it happened and it cannot be changed now. "Feel" means to feel good about yourself, knowing you did your best and made the right decisions, whether they worked out well or not. "Feel" means you are moving on to your next challenge.

- **Think**

This is where you begin the process of revising your strategy for the remainder of the hole based on what just happened. You had a strategy for the shot you just hit. Now, from the perspective of where your ball was moments ago, you can start to shape a new strategy going forward. "Think" means to learn something from this shot that can help the next one. "Think" means to assess whether you properly accounted for the factors that influenced this shot, including those things you thought of in your pre-shot routine. "Think" means to remember to flip the switch off and enjoy your environment. It is time to move on to your next shot.

2. Time Travel

One of the challenges of focus is to stay in the present moment. Getting out of the moment is what I call "time travel." You can travel back in time (at least, you can in your mind) and worry and fret over things that happened in the past. Hopefully, you can learn from your mistakes, but there is no need to carry the emotional baggage of past holes or rounds with you.

Those things that happened in the past (that 3-putt, your poor tee shot, etc.) are done and gone. They are ancient history, even if they happened only moments ago. They cannot be changed. They must be accepted because they are a part of your current situation.

Notice how traveling back in time is usually about reliving poor shots? Oh how we love to carry those memories around with us, but they do us no good. The one exception to this is to recall a *good* memory. Remembering great shots can help you in your pre-shot routine by front-loading positive feelings about your choice of shot and club selection.

You can also travel into the future and imagine all of the wonderful or terrible things that might happen. You might need to par the final three holes to win, or to shoot your best round. Or, you might be thinking about and dreading an upcoming hole that has been difficult for you. Both of these forms of time travel only serve to increase your perceived pressure to perform the only act that matters: your current shot. They both cause you to lose focus on the present.

A Golf MasterMind sheds unpleasant memories, shuns thoughts of the future, and shines in the present. This concept of "time travel" leads to the next major challenge of focus that I call "uncontrollables."

3. Uncontrollables

The world of golf is full of things that shape your thoughts and actions. You can control some of these. Many are uncontrollable. All of them are potential distractions that can cause you to lose focus at the critical moments during your pre-shot or in-shot routines.

I think golfers tend to be highly controlling people. After all, it is our main objective to control our ball. We seek to control how far it goes, how high it flies, how it curves (or doesn't), where it lands, how much it rolls, etc. Frequently, we also seek to control all of the things around us that might have an impact on our success in achieving this impossible objective.

When it is time to hit your ball, you need to clear your mind of these distractions and focus. But how? I think the answer is simple, but the solution is quite difficult.

Think about the things that are happening. The wind is blowing. The fairways are soaked from a recent rain. The golf course is playing much longer than you expected. Your fellow competitors are hitting drives much farther than yours. That other player has a weird swing. Your ball ends up in a terrible lie in deep grass just a few feet from the green. The water hazard extends much farther into the fairway in front of the green than you thought. Why did you 3-putt that last green?

What can you do about these things?

Nothing.

Actually, there is one thing that you can do about these and all other "uncontrollables." You can love them and accept them as they are. I understand – you think that I am crazy for suggesting that you love these awful and unfair bad breaks and outrageous strokes of bad luck that you in no way deserve. And, you are at least partially correct. They are awful. They are unfair. They are bad. They are outrageous. It was bad luck. You definitely don't deserve what happened.

But they happened.

And you cannot change them.

And I'm not crazy.

So, consider your options if you don't want to love and accept these and other uncontrollables:

- You can rant.
- You can rave.
- You can complain.
- You can shout.
- You can curse.
- You can throw your club.
- You can act like a fool.
- You can let it bother you for a few holes.

But none of these things will change what happened. So, you really have no choice but to accept the uncontrollables. I suggest that you go beyond acceptance and love them, for they add spice and interest and challenge to the game. Without uncontrollables, golf would be boring and easy. What fun would that be?

Accepting uncontrollables means to think to yourself how lucky you are to be able to demonstrate your ability to focus on what you *can* control.

And what should you do about those things that you can control?

Control them.

Think positive thoughts.

Be optimistic.

Practice with intent.

Take a deep breath.

Have a strategy.

Swing with commitment.

Laugh.

Have a positive attitude.

This final suggestion is perhaps the most important, because your attitude has arguably the greatest influence on your level of performance. As the late PGA Tour star Payne Stewart said, "A bad attitude is worse than a bad swing."

If you let the uncontrollables bother and distract you, you have little chance to succeed. If you accept their presence, love the challenge they represent, and file them away in your cabinet of "learning experiences," you can move on with purposeful intent.

That to me is the essence of focus: your ability to change those things that you can control and ignore those things that you cannot, allowing you to proceed with your mission of making your best possible effort on the shot at hand.

It will not always be easy to do this, but it is even more difficult to struggle against the uncontrollables. After all of your futile efforts and all of the energy you will waste doing so, your golf ball will still be sitting there, looking up at you and waiting to be sent off to a better destination. It deserves your best shot.

The list of controllables and uncontrollables is probably endless, but the following table should help you recognize some of them. No doubt, seeing them categorized like this makes them seem obvious. However, studying this list can help you remember which is which when you are on the course in the heat of the moment.

Things I Can Control	Things I Cannot Control
How I feel about the weather	The weather
How much I train/prepare	The competition
What I say	What other players say
What I think	What other players think
How I feel	How other players feel
How I react to things	How others react to things
My swing	Another player's swing
What I do before swinging	What other players do
What I do after swinging	Where my ball ends up
How far I hit the ball	How far others hit the ball
How I act toward others	How others treat me
My course knowledge	Where the hazards are
My knowledge of the rules	The rules of golf
My strategy	How long the course plays
My ability to recover	The lie of my ball
What I choose to think about	The footprint in the bunker
My mood	Golf course conditions
My attitude	My prior shot
My emotions	Holes already played
What I am doing now	What happened 1 second ago
What I eat	The past
What I drink	The future

A Golf MasterMind recognizes those things that he or she can control and handles them as necessary, and accepts, ignores and loves those things that he or she cannot control.

4. Emotional Management

The discussion of uncontrollables leads naturally to the issue of emotional control, and indeed "my emotions" is listed as a "thing you can control" in the above table. The dictionary defines control as "to hold in restraint; to check." Essentially, controlling your emotions means to restrain or suppress them, or to keep them inside you and not express them.

However, I'm not so sure that your emotions really can be 100% controlled. I'm also not sure that they *should* be suppressed. So, in terms of their effect on your ability to focus at the critical pre-shot and in-shot times, and to be able to think clearly about your strategy for your shot, I call this issue "emotional management" instead of "emotional control."

During every round of golf, you will have emotions, both good and bad. They will surface before you even realize you are having them. A Golf MasterMind will find a productive and acceptable way in which he or she can express them, and shift the destructive emotions to ones that can be controlled and used in a positive way. In this case, "productive" means to allow the emotion to happen and to pass.

Emotions, especially anger, happen like a wave (or perhaps more like a tsunami). Something occurs (your ball sliced out of bounds) that triggers the emotion (anger), which rises quickly to a crest (curses shouted, club pounded), then it slowly (lasting for several more shots) subsides until it washes away your round and leaves you emotionally exhausted and in a state of acceptance and calm.

Emotional events can also be triggered by external factors, such as something another player says or does, or even something a spectator says or does. As a golf parent and "daddy caddy," I know that I have said and done things that have sent my son into an emotional tailspin. If this happens to you, you must manage yourself and keep these emotional events from distracting you from your game.

The goal of emotional management is to recognize the rising wave and decrease both its height and duration. You want to be able to survive its peak and regain your focus for the next shot. In my book "Daddy Caddy on the Bag," I called this "let 1=1." This means to let one bad shot cost you only one stroke (or less), not more than one stroke. It means to accept what happened, get over it, and move on to your next shot.

Again, the key is recognition. Emotions like anger, anxiety, fear, and even hope affect your body chemistry and your ability to control your muscles. These emotions make it difficult or impossible to make your normal golf swing. They also invade your mental processes and make it almost impossible to think clearly and rationally. In other words, they may take control of your body before you even realize it. Your only hope is recognition: see and feel it coming, and act before it is too late.

What can you do to avoid the emotional tsunami? Think of it like this: a real tsunami is only a large swell, and it travels through deep water without effect. If you were on a boat in the middle of the ocean, you would not even know it had passed. It is only when the land rises up and fights against the swell and the sea becomes shallow that the swell becomes a tsunami, as the mound of water has nowhere to go but up into a giant wave. Once it peaks, it has no choice but to crash onto the shore. Its energy must be dissipated somehow.

As you feel a negative emotion such as anger swelling up inside you, would you rather stay on the beach and fight it, or move out to deep water and let it pass? Don't fight it. It is okay to get angry. But, take action to derail the anger before it defeats you:

- Acknowledge your emotion (whether anger, anxiety, or other). Destructive emotions (see below) are your enemy, and once you recognize them, you can defeat them.

- Take a long, deep breath and hold it for a few seconds (more on this later also).

- Tell yourself that you are not going to allow this emotion to take control over you. You are in charge.

- Again, don't fight or try to suppress the emotion. It needs to be acknowledged and released.

- Breathe. You are okay. You are stronger than this emotion, and it is not going to control you. You have unfinished golf business to do, and your destructive emotion is not invited.

In dealing with your emotions, you should seek a neutral, healthy coherent state of mind (your "inner game") that will allow your body to perform to its physical "outer game" potential. By coherent, I mean a harmonious synchronization of your mental, physical, and emotional systems. When these systems are coherent, you feel a sense of wisdom and harmony and are primed to perform almost subconsciously at your highest level.

I think this is what we refer to as the "zone." And, I further believe that we should try to create this coherence and allow the zone to happen. You may not always be in the zone, but the closer you can get, and the longer you can stay there, the better you will play.

But how can you do it?

Before I go any further, I want to give some examples of playing in the zone. Perhaps you have been there. If not, you undoubtedly will at some point, even if it only lasts for a few holes. It goes like this.

I was caddying (yes again for my son), who was playing in a one-day local tournament. He had been playing well, but nothing spectacular. He began with a birdie on the opening hole, a par five, and followed with a nice par save on the second hole. He followed that with a solid par on the third hole. Then, he three-putted the fourth, missing a 30-inch par putt. Nothing spectacular so far, but he was upset. In fact, I think he felt his round was ruined. Somehow, he shrugged off the bogey and was determined to make it up.

And then, for reasons unknown, he entered the zone.

Threading the needle with his tee shot, he left himself 195 yards to the hole on the fifth hole, a par 5. He ripped a perfect 3-wood to three feet, and holed the putt for eagle. He then proceeded to birdie the next four holes for a 6-under par 30 on the front nine. Somehow, the hole looked like a garbage can to him, and he couldn't miss. And somehow, life returned to normal beginning on the tenth hole. He finished with a great round of 67, but afterward it was clear that he had entered and then left the zone.

Before the zone, his golf was normal. In it, he was unconscious. After it, things were a bit of a struggle. What changed? Was it the long walk to the tenth tee, where he began thinking about how well he was playing (out of his time zone)? Was it the botched chip and poor bogey on the tenth (anger)? The missed easy birdie putt on the eleventh (frustration)? Whatever the cause, the zone came and went.

I've been in the zone too. Most recently, I was out for a fun round with a friend. I hadn't played or practiced much, so my expectations were low, and the course was tough. My mindset was one of enjoyment at just being out on the course, with no self-imposed pressure to shoot any particular score. We only had time for nine holes.

And I shot a cool 4-under par 32, hitting eight greens in regulation and putting better than I have in recent memory. My recovery shot on the one missed green was tour-quality, even though my short game was rusty. I relate this experience not to expose my incredible golf game (it isn't), but because it was one of those days where I seemed able to do no wrong. I could feel that I was in the zone, and golf was unbelievably easy.

In the zone, I was emotionally neutral. I visualized my shots and somehow my body made them happen. I was coherent. In your quest to find the elusive zone, you will need to manage your emotions to achieve coherence.

Let's take a look at a list of emotions and see which are aligned with the zone and which are destructive. Since they are certainly more prevalent on the golf course, and more apt to distract our focus, let's begin with the destructive emotions:

Destructive Emotions

- Anger – ranging from mild irritation (missing the fairway) to intense rage (chunking your ball into the hazard).

- Anxiety – your overwhelming sense of apprehension, marked by physiological signs such as sweating, tension, and increased pulse (such as when teeing off on the first hole in front of several groups of golfers, or standing over that three foot putt needed to shoot your best score).

- Boredom – loss of interest between shots, perhaps due to slow play.

- Distracted – mentally confused and unsure of what to do, such as uncertainty in selecting a strategy, choosing a club, evaluating the conditions, picking a line of putt, etc..

- Disappointed – feeling as though you have not performed up to your personal standards.

- Envy – as you watch your fellow competitor hit prodigious drives, knock the flag down with laser approach shots, and somehow save par from everywhere.

- Fear – including fear of failure (hitting a poor shot), fear of embarrassment in front of others, and even fear of success.

- Frustration – due to your inability to do what you believe to be simple and easy: control your golf ball.

- Hope – thinking of the future and wishing for that great final score, that trophy, and your acceptance speech… before you have finished your round.

- Self pity – feeling sorry for yourself due to adverse situations such as bad breaks, bad bounces, and bumpy greens where you cannot accept and cope with the situation.

These destructive emotions all distract you from your goal of playing your best golf. They certainly make the game less enjoyable (for both you and everyone around you).

Then there are those emotions compatible with the zone:

Zone-Enabling Emotions

- Happiness – that deep feeling of contentment, love, satisfaction, pleasure, or joy that you might get just from being on the golf course (instead of at work), and enjoying being with friends.

- Optimism – expecting the best of possible outcomes, and thinking positively that you can hit the needed shot, recover from adversity, or play your best when it counts.

- Relaxed – free from worry or anxiety, including not even seeing or recognizing obstacles and hazards that are in play, but which would not affect a well-struck shot.

- Trust – firm belief in your ability to perform when it counts as well as you have done in practice.

- Calm – your lack of emotion and ability to ignore external events that would otherwise bother or distract you.

- Comfortable – free from stress or anxiety, such as your ability to accept whatever happens to your ball and your score.

- Confident – faith and trust that you will act correctly and achieve your objective.

Clearly, you will never play your best golf while you are experiencing one or more of the "destructive emotions." And clearly, these "zone-enabling emotions" are highly desirable, and you should seek to replace destructive emotions with zone-enabling emotions wherever and whenever possible.

But once again, how can you do it?

As I alluded above in the recommendation to breathe, I think the answer lies in HeartMath. What is HeartMath and how does it work? First, some background.

Studies have found that people in a coherent state (i.e. where their heart rhythm pattern is smooth and orderly) are noticeably able to improve their thinking and performance, whether they are making decisions or playing sports. When your heart rhythm is coherent (smooth and orderly), you are able to access higher-thinking centers in your brain, so you can think more clearly and see more options or solutions to problems. When your heart becomes incoherent, this access becomes inhibited and you are likely to find your reactions are slower and you are not able to think so clearly.

HeartMath is the science of synchronizing your heart rhythm with your brain, and the HeartMath Institute has developed ways you can accomplish this, even in the heat of competition.

For example, here is how the HeartMath Institute describes the process of managing the anger emotion:

We all have a pattern of how we have dealt with anger in the past. This pattern is imprinted on our brain, and it is difficult to change, so even though we try, when an anger-triggering situation comes up again, our old pattern takes over with the same old anger.

What does it take to change this pattern? It is more than just relaxation or cognitive techniques. It takes the power of the heart.

What does this mean — the "power of the heart?" Researchers John and Beatrice Lacey (1970) showed that the heart's nervous system relays important information back to the brain. The HeartMath Institute took this revelation a step further to discover an extraordinary reciprocal relationship between heart "intelligence" and higher cognitive functions. They found that negative emotions create jagged and disordered heart rhythms, which in turn trigger increased levels of emotional distress. Conversely, people who learn to generate balanced, coherent heart rhythms find themselves far more balanced emotionally.

HeartMath gives you tools to slow down your emotional reactions so the old patterns and anger reflexes stop controlling you.

The HeartMath system is a scientifically validated way to reduce stress, and more importantly, to transform the negative emotional and physiological effects that occur when you experience feelings of stress or a stressful event. HeartMath is different from other stress relieving activities like listening to music because those activities take place after the event has passed. By the time you wind down, you've already experienced the harmful, often unpleasant effects of stress. The stress hormone cortisol, for example, stays in your system for hours once it is released in to your system. High levels of stress hormones can have a serious negative impact on your physical health. So the key appears to be learning how to transform your reaction to stress, and therefore stop the emotional and hormonal fallout that follows.

By using HeartMath techniques, you can change your reaction to the destructive emotions, minimize their strength, and shorten their duration. Unfortunately, I am not able to provide instructions on how to do this, but the process is simple. Although it does require practice, virtually anyone will find that they are able to achieve coherence. As a certified HeartMath Coach/Mentor, I have demonstrated this capability in myself and others. HeartMath can be an extremely effective solution to managing your emotions and finding the elusive zone.

Measuring Your Ability to Focus

How well do you focus when it is time to "flip the switch" and hit your golf ball? How well do you manage your emotions? Like everything, you must have a way to know where you are now in order to be able to improve. What if you could see a direct correlation between emotional events and lost strokes? What if you could see the relationship between using your pre-shot and post-shot routines and your scores?

The following example Golf MasterMind Focus-Ability Scorecard can help you evaluate your focus skills and see where distractions may be costing you strokes. I have completed an example to show how you can use the scorecard, and also included a blank scorecard in Appendix 1 for you to use. You can also find the Golf MasterMind Focus-Ability Scorecard in the Golf MasterMind Workbook.

GOLF MASTERMIND "FOCUS-ABILITY" SCORECARD

		Hole	1	2	3	4	5	6	7	8	9	10	11	12	13	14	15	16	17	18	Tot
Date: EXAMPLE		Par	5	3	4	4	4	3	5	4	4	3	4	4	3	4	5	4	5	4	72
Course: *My Golf Course*		Score	5	4	6	5	4	3	5	6	3	3	4	4	5	5	4	4	6	5	81
		Relation to Par		1	2	1				2	-1				2	1	-1		1	1	9
		Bounce-Back					X				X			X			X				4
Emotional Events		Anger		X	X								X								3
		Anxiety																	X	X	2
		Distracted													X						1
		Frustrated														X					1
		Other																			0
Time Management Skills		Pre-Shot TFA	X	X						X	X	X		X		X					7
		Post-Shot AFT	X	X							X	X		X		X					6

How to Use the Golf MasterMind Focus-Ability Scorecard

Refer to the above example scorecard:

1. **Date and Course**: Record the date of your round and the name of the golf course you played.

2. **Par**: Fill in the pars for all 18 holes. Note that the scorecard does not have a subtotal for nine holes. This is so you can look for patterns across the completed card without an interruption in the middle of the round. Record the pars in the order in which you played the golf course. If you started on a hole other than #1, use that starting hole as your first hole, and record the pars from that point on the scorecard.

3. **Score**: Record your actual score for each hole, along with the total score. Record your scores in the order in which you played the golf course, matching the pars as recorded above. That is, if you started on hole #10, then that is your first hole, and your score would be recorded in the box for hole #1 on the scorecard.

4. **Relation to Par**: Compare your score to par on each hole and record the number in the box. An eagle is -2, a birdie is -1, a par is blank (don't write anything in the box for a par), a bogey is 1, a double-bogey is 2, etc. Add these numbers and record them in the total column. Double-check your math to ensure that your actual score (81 in the example) matches your Relation to Par (9). This checks, because 81 is 9-over par of 72.

   How to Interpret: Your relation to par can move in patterns that can reveal many aspects of your focus during a round. Leaving the par boxes blank can help you see these patterns. First, you can look at groups of numbers, such as in the example where over par holes can be seen to come two or three at a time. You can also look at the opening four holes, the middle ten holes, and the closing four holes (the opening and closing four boxes are shaded on the scorecard). Perhaps you are nervous as you begin, and find yourself over par early in the round. Perhaps you are anxious during the closing holes, hoping to finish well. In the example, two finishing pars would have allowed you to break 80. Ideally, you should not see any patterns in your relation to par. Over par holes should occur randomly and not be related to each other. If you see any patterns, you can work with your PGA or LPGA professional to discuss the causes and identify solutions.

5. **Bounce-Back**: Write an "X" in the box any time your "Relation to Par" is par or better and the prior two holes are both bogey or worse. Also write an "X" if your score is par or better and the prior hole is double-bogey or worse. You can also record an "X" any time you feel you overcame a problem that arose on the prior hole, even if the prior hole was a par or better. In the example, the 12th hole was a par, but the 11th hole (also a par) "should have been" a birdie because you missed a two-foot putt. Therefore, you overcame anger on the 11th hole and "bounced back" to make a par on 12. Use your judgment on where to give yourself credit for recovering from an emotional challenge and coming back strong.

    How to Interpret: The "bounce-back" factor helps you see when you have "righted the ship" after a bad hole, as shown in the example on the 9th hole. As described, a bad hole doesn't always mean a bad score; it could be a wasted stroke where you didn't capitalize on an opportunity (such as reaching the green in two shots on a par 5, then 3-putting for par). A bad hole could also be one where you had an emotional event; record the bounce-back if you didn't let that event affect your play on the following hole.

6. **Emotional Events**: Write an "X" in the box for any hole where you believe that you had an emotional reaction. Write the "X" in the

appropriate row, associated with the type of Emotional Event (Anger, Anxiety, Distracted, Frustrated, or Other).

How to Interpret: Look for a correlation between your emotional event and your score, either on the hole where the emotion happened or on subsequent holes. For example, you may be able to see where your anger on one hole carried forward and led to one or more additional bad holes, such as shown in the example on holes 2 and 3.

7. **Time Management Skills**: Write an "X" in the box for any hole where you used your pre-shot TFA (think, feel, act) and post-shot AFT (act, feel, think) routines *on every shot* on that hole.

How to Interpret: Look for a correlation between following your planned pre-shot and post-shot routines and your scores. Also look for lapses in using your routines, and try to increase your usage on subsequent rounds. Even if you do not see a correlation, you can use the time management section to focus on the process you are following. Even if your scoring results are not satisfactory, you can achieve your objectives of following your intended routines. Strive to score 18 on both your pre-shot and post-shot routine usage.

You may be surprised to find that just the act of recording your scores on the Golf MasterMind Focus-Ability Scorecard will probably help you play better. In physics, this is called the "observer effect," where the act of observing something changes its behavior. In this case, knowing that you will have to mark down each emotional event will change how you handle that event (hopefully for the better, as described above). The act of having to record whether you remember to use your pre-shot and post-shot routines will help you remember to do them.

Therefore, to help you get a baseline starting point for your focusing skills, think back to a recent round and complete a scorecard by memory before you begin to use the scorecard for a new round.

Although even just one round can reveal much about your "focus-ability," you will get the greatest benefit if you keep a notebook or spreadsheet with your Golf MasterMind Focus-Ability Scorecard data for multiple rounds. Then, you will be able to identify patterns and track your improvement over time.

•　　　•　　　•

We golfers spend our time on the links in three basic ways. Nearly 80% of our time is spent riding (or, preferably, walking) from one shot to the next, hopefully relaxing and enjoying being outdoors. Around 20% of our time is spent strategizing and thinking about hitting our golf ball. Only 1% of our time is spent actually swinging and hitting the ball. When we think of golf this way, the paradox is clear. We spend hundreds of hours practicing, taking lessons, and perfecting our swing for less than three minutes of action in a five hour round of golf.

Those three minutes will either make or break our round, so it is of critical importance that we use them to the best of our ability. Our challenge is to focus during the strategizing and thinking time so that we can apply our ball-striking skills to the best of our abilities. Focus in golf, then is the point where the critical factors of time management, time travel, uncontrollables, and emotional management come together when it is time to hit the ball.

A Golf MasterMind has the ability to relax during the between-shot time and "flip the switch" and focus during the pre-shot and in-shot times. He or she stays in the present, and isn't distracted by external events that cannot be controlled. Most important, a Golf MasterMind manages his or her emotions to achieve mental, physical, and emotional coherence when it matters the most.

CHAPTER FIVE

"Of all of the hazards, fear is the worst."

— Sam Snead

Confidence

Our climb up the Peak Performance Pyramid began with dreams and goals (motivation), passed through practical skills (ability), traveled through the thoughtful mind (strategy), and climbed through emotions (focus). Now, we must ascend to the spiritual peak of confidence. I say this final level is spiritual not because I am a particularly spiritual person but because confidence is all about faith, trust, and self-belief. Ironically, these spiritual concepts are rooted in the practical, because confidence is based on competence.

In order for you to accomplish something, you must have faith that you can do it. You must trust and truly believe in yourself and your ability to accomplish it. Only you can know whether you have the necessary skills and abilities. And only you can fill yourself with the confidence needed to push through the challenges and difficulties you will face along the way. Interestingly, in this way the discussion of confidence circles back to the beginning level of motivation.

Indeed, the process of striving for peak performance is circular, and confidence pervades each level.

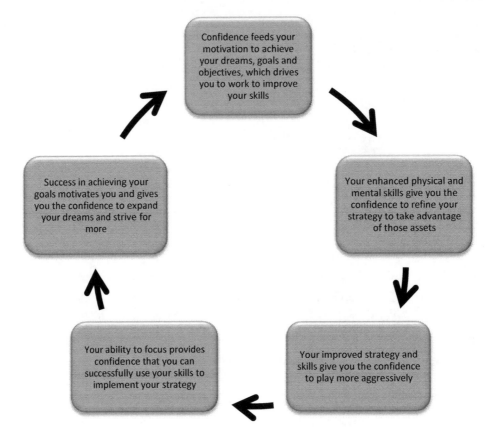

It is important to understand that your level of confidence should not be related to your skill level or your ability to play golf. You can be confident that you are able to play to your ability. You can be confident that you can develop a successful strategy for your game. You can be confident that you can focus and control your emotions. And, you can be confident by not placing too much importance on the outcome of a round of golf or a tournament and not worrying about your score or what others might think of your performance.

A fortunate element of confidence is that it can be a self-fulfilling prophecy. You can succeed simply because you are confident – and you can fail simply because you lack it. Thus, given its importance, there is every reason to find ways to believe in yourself.

Referring back to the NCAA coaches' responses regarding mental toughness, the top two most important characteristics sought by college coaches were:

1. Having an unshakable self-belief in your ability to achieve your competition goals; and

2. Having an unshakable self-belief that you possess unique qualities and abilities that make you better than your opponents.

In other words, college coaches know successful athletes believe in themselves and that their belief is unshakable. Exactly what is meant by unshakable? Unshakable is:

-   Unwavering – solid and steady, with no doubts.

-   Steadfast – persistent and committed, with dedication.

-   Constant – stable and reliable; never giving up.

-   Immovable – permanent and set, with no changes.

-   Resolute – stubborn and determined, with tenacity.

-   Stanch – unbendable and firm, with unyielding commitment.

It isn't easy to imagine a more powerful adjective than "unshakable." The NCAA coaches know how difficult it can be to pursue dreams while also living the life of a college student athlete. For them and for their students' success, they know that an elite golfer must believe in himself or herself, and that their belief must be unshakable.

How can you build unshakable self confidence? There are four ways: through competence, experience, success, and positivity.

Competence

Confidence ultimately comes from the intersection of the lower levels of the Peak Performance Pyramid. If you know you can focus and play to the level of your ability, you will have confidence. If you have hit hundreds of successful flop shots over practice bunkers, you will be confident as you address your ball to hit that shot on the final hole of a tournament.

On the other hand, if you are attempting a shot strategy that is not supported by your skills and which you don't believe you can hit successfully, you will lack confidence. If you dream of playing college golf but don't put in the practice time, your skills will suffer and you will not believe that you can play to that level – and you won't.

There is no substitute for competence. You either have the skills necessary to play to the level you intend, or you don't. I confess I have attempted many shots where I hoped for a good result, knowing that I was perhaps trying for a bit too much. There may be no worse feeling than a lack of confidence over the ball, and you can't count on lady luck every time.

The answer is to match your strategy with your skills. You must believe that you can execute the intended shot, and that belief comes from competence. And, competence comes from hard work, practice, and knowledge of your capabilities.

Experience

Competence gives you the skills and abilities, but you need real on-course competitive experience applying them if you are to build confidence. As an example, a young golfer recently competed in his first tournament. He had hit thousands of practice balls on the range and had played dozens of practice rounds. However, he had never experienced the feeling you get when the starter introduces you on the first tee of a tournament.

Even though he had lots of experience playing golf, he had no real competitive experience. He was so nervous and fearful that he could hardly swing his club as he hit that opening tee shot. He lacked confidence.

Another young golfer has played in well over 100 tournaments. When she steps to the first tee and hears her name, her competitive fire is lit and she swings with confidence and self-assuredness. She's "been there, done that" so many times that she is ready with her best game from that first swing on.

There is no substitute for experience, and it can only be had by having it. In Chapter 1 on motivation, I wrote that one of the solutions to getting confidence is through realistic practice sessions, where you simulate competitive conditions and create pressure to perform. Although this is extremely helpful in making practice more like the real game of golf, it is still far from the reality of playing when it matters. Tournament experience gives you the confidence to relax and be yourself, and to take full advantage of your competence.

Success

Although competence and experience are necessary in order to have confidence, they are not sufficient. You must also have some success. This does not mean that you have to have won a tournament in order to have confidence. There are many ways to have success that do not involve winning. You can be successful by:

- Achieving one or more of your objectives.

- Achieving one or more of your larger goals.

- Recovering from mistakes.

- Hitting a memorable great shot.

- Seeing progress and improvement on any of the Golf MasterMind worksheets.

- Implementing and sticking with your strategy.

- Meeting your process objectives (such as using your pre-shot routine).

- Managing your emotions.

These successes, whether large or small, provide concrete evidence that you have the competence needed to succeed. They allow you to believe in yourself and trust in your abilities for future situations. Ultimately, you yourself are the source of your own self confidence. That confidence comes from knowing that you have the ability to succeed and from having proven it in the past.

Positivity

Lastly, confidence comes from having a positive attitude. Golf is a challenging game, and you will not always be successful. In fact, your successes will be greatly outnumbered by your "others." I call them "others" because they are not failures. You are not a failure if you do not win. As above, there are many ways to succeed, both large and small. You must maintain a positive attitude and search for the successes, however small, in yourself and in everything you do.

You will make mistakes, but they will only be important if you make them so. Your attitude about your mistakes is what matters, and if you take a positive approach to them, they are a least recoverable and at most a valuable learning experience.

•   •   •

A Golf MasterMind remains positive and optimistic about the future, and believes in his or her own abilities to succeed. This confidence comes from competence, and from matching expectations to his or her skills and abilities. Confidence comes from experience and remaining positive in searching for successes, both small and large. And it comes from following the Golf MasterMind system and choosing to act like a pro.

CHAPTER SIX

"Being a Golf MasterMind Pro isn't hard. You just have decide whether you want to or not."

- Rick Heard

The Golf MasterMind Pro

What is a Golf MasterMind Pro? It is someone who:

- Has an intense inner drive to succeed and who will let nothing get in the way of achieving his or her goals.

- Can make the most of his or her existing physical golf skills, and will practice with intent to improve in the most important areas.

- Is tough-minded and resilient, and ignores temporary setbacks.

- Knows that he or she is not perfect, and can accept poor shots and leave them in the past.

- Sees failures as opportunities to learn and grow, and can convert them into future successes.

- Knows his or her game and capabilities, and develops a plan of attack for each hole that maximizes the chances to score.

- Can "flip the switch" and focus on the task and shot at hand, yet can enjoy the time between shots.

- Doesn't let his or her emotions interfere with performance.

- Believes in his or her ability to succeed.

How would you like to play a money match against a Golf MasterMind Pro? No doubt, he or she would be a very tough opponent.

You are probably not a Golf MasterMind Pro right now, but regardless of your golf experience, your skill level, or your golf handicap, you are somewhere on the Golf MasterMind spectrum. If you are motivated, you too can be a Golf MasterMind Pro. You do not need any particular ball-striking skills. You do not need to be able to break par. You do not need a great short game. You only need to want to be one. The first step is finding out where you are now.

Where Are You on the Golf MasterMind Spectrum?

Since you are a golfer, you are somewhere on the Golf MasterMind spectrum. Remember that you can be a Golf MasterMind Pro no matter what level of golf skill you possess – you only need to make the most of your golf abilities and strive to improve. To help you understand what that means, you can assess your own level of agreement with the following statements of Golf MasterMind traits.

These are distinguishing characteristics and qualities that I believe are important and that are representative of the philosophies and beliefs behind being a Golf MasterMind Pro. With an honest self-assessment of your agreement with each statement, you can evaluate your own strengths and opportunities for improvement on the key elements of the Peak Performance Pyramid: Motivation, Ability, Strategy, Focus, and Confidence.

Think carefully as you read the statements and decide whether you agree with and behave according to each one. Remember, there is no "right" or "wrong" response to any of the statements. Your behavior might agree strongly with some traits and it might not agree at all with others. Most important, remember that your responses are *yours*, not anyone else's, including your parents, your siblings, and your friends.

I am confident that if you truly believe in and act according to these traits, you will make positive changes in your physical and mental game that will lower your golf scores and move you toward becoming a Golf MasterMind Pro.

Motivation – My Inner Desire to Excel

- I have a dream. I can envision myself living that dream in the future.

- I know what I have to do to move toward my dream, and I set challenging goals for myself to help me get there. My goals are achievable, but I know I will need to work hard to accomplish them. I know that if I achieve my goals, I will be closer to realizing my dream.

- I write down my personal goals for what I want to achieve in golf. I keep these in a conspicuous place where I can see them every day.

- I have a strong desire to compete, perform well, and win. I am willing to make sacrifices so that I can be the best.

- I enjoy the thrill of competition. I get excited to compete in tournaments, and competition motivates me to practice harder. I love the feeling of pressure and excitement that I feel when I am competing.

- I enjoy practicing my short game and putting. I know that this is the most important part of my scoring ability and I feel that I can save par from almost anywhere.

- The more I practice, the better I get. I see and feel a direct benefit from practice, because my swing gets more consistent, my game improves, and I gain confidence.

- I play golf for me, not for my parents or anyone else. I know that my parents and others are proud of my golf abilities, but I play because I love how it makes me feel.

- No matter how well I play, I feel great about myself, and others feel great about me. Even when I play poorly, I am still a great person and my family still loves me.

Motivation – My Mental Toughness and My Ability to Overcome Setbacks

- When I have a bad hole, I frequently score much better on the next hole. I can leave that bad experience in the past and move on with optimism and confidence.

- I bounce back from setbacks and do not get too discouraged. I know that golf is extremely challenging and that everything will not always go as planned. I view those setbacks as opportunities for me to show off my skills and ability to recover and move on.

- I find enjoyment from difficult situations because they let me create shots to escape from the trouble.

- I handle criticism well and use it to my advantage. Even if I disagree with my critics, I don't get defensive and I recognize that there could be some truth to their opinion. I can accept the criticism and use it as a positive opportunity to improve.

- I know that bad shots or holes are my responsibility, and not because of someone or something other than myself. I can accept that I am not perfect and move on to the next shot without blaming others.

- I am stubborn. I don't give up easily and I have a strong belief in myself and my abilities.

Ability – Ball-Striking, Ball Control, and Knowledge of My Game

- I practice ball control, and strive to be able to hit any type of shot. I practice trouble shots, recovery shots, uneven lies, difficult situations, and ball control so that I am ready for any situation on the course.

- I know my strengths and weaknesses and I focus my practice sessions on my greatest opportunities for improvement.

- I know exactly how far I can carry the ball with every club in almost any circumstance. I also know my consistency factor, or my expected degree of error with each club.

- I know that I need to putt well in order to shoot low scores. I devote at least 40% of my practice time to putting.

- I listen to others when they give me advice on my swing or my game. I know that there are many philosophies about the golf swing and how to play, and I can learn from everyone as I build my own game.

Strategy – Using My Abilities to Play My Best

- I prepare a game plan for each course and each hole. I know that there is a "best" way for me to play every hole. I plan my strategy ahead of time in practice rounds and by studying the course layout, not while I am playing during the round.

- I stick with my game plan no matter how others play the hole or shot. I don't let what others are doing or how they are playing change what I intend to do.

- I stick to my game plan during a round even if I'm not playing the way I hoped to play. I know that my game plan for future holes is my best plan, even if I haven't played well. Also, if I am playing well I still stick to my game plan and not become defensive or too conservative on the remaining holes.

- I think about the risks and rewards and assess my probability of success on each shot. I don't try shots that are risky or unrealistic based on my abilities. I want to select the shot that gives me the best expected outcome (lowest expected score) based on what I know I can realistically do.

- I aim at the smallest target I can find. Even with a wide-open fairway, I know that I still need to pick a specific target and aim at it.

- I hit good shots into places or situations that make my next shot easy for me. I think about where I want to leave my ball for my next shot to give me the easiest angle and the best opportunity to score.

Focus – Applying My Skills, Abilities, and Strategy

- I use my Think-Feel-Act preshot routine and my Act-Feel-Think post-shot routine – every time.

- I commit to my choice of club, my shot, my read of the green, my target, and my strategy and don't change my mind while over the ball. If I do have doubts about my shot, I back off and begin my routine again.

- I block out the crowd, other players, and other distractions during my round. I have a way of "flipping the switch" and focusing when it is my turn to play, and I don't even notice what is going on around me.

- I remember to eat and drink water during a round. I know that proper hydration and nutrition is important in order for me to focus and play my best.

- I think about or focus on where I want my ball to go. Once I assess the risks and rewards of my intended shot, I do not think about where I don't want my ball to go.

- I love to play quickly, but I don't let slow play bother me or make me play worse.

- I trust my swing mechanics and do not think about them while I am hitting the ball.

- No one could guess how well I am playing by watching how I act. I carry myself and remain composed even when things aren't going well, because I can accept what happened and focus on my next shot.

- I play better in competition than I do in practice or "regular" rounds. I am able to elevate my game when it matters and rise to the occasion when it really counts.

- I play without knowing exactly how I stand and what my score is. I can get into the "zone" and play unconsciously.

- After a bad shot, I remain calm and avoid saying or doing something bad in anger. I know that don't have to like my shot, and I can accept it for what it is and not let it bother me. I know that outbursts of anger and emotion will not help me on my next shot, and I know that my prior shots have nothing to do with how well I will hit my next shot.

- After a bad shot, I can move on without analyzing or worrying about what went wrong with my swing. I know that I'm not perfect and I can accept whatever happened and not carry my bad shot with me as I move on.

- I remember to use HeartMath or other techniques when I need to gather myself and regain focus. I can sense when I'm beginning to lose focus and control, and I act quickly to regain coherence.

- When I finish my round, I reflect on what I did well and where I could have improved. I strive to identify "lost strokes" and to determine what happened and what I would do differently on my next round. As I think about the reasons for lost strokes, I identify those within my control (e.g., strategy, focus, confidence) and those simply due to mis-hits.

Confidence – My Belief in Myself and My Ability to Perform

- I feel positive about my abilities in competition. I know that my practice, preparation, strategy, and skills will enable me to play my best.

- Under pressure, I am able to make decisions with confidence and commitment. I trust in my abilities.

- I interpret potential threats as positive opportunities. I know that everyone will face difficult situations and that my skills will give me an advantage.

- I love playing in bad weather (wind, rain, cold, heat, etc.) because it gives me an advantage over the other players.

- I feel in control of my performance. I know that my golf score is up to me.

- I have unshakable confidence in my ability. No matter how difficult things might become, I know that I can find a way to succeed.

- I give myself a boost with thoughts that are positive and encouraging. I am my own best friend and fan.

After reviewing these statements of Golf MasterMind traits, you will have an idea where you are on the Golf MasterMind spectrum. Most likely, you will find that you are strong in some areas and have opportunities for improvement in others. The point of reviewing the Golf MasterMind traits is to help you find those improvement opportunities and work on them with the goal of climbing to the peak of the Peak Performance Pyramid.

As you read the statements, think about the ones that your behaviors and actions do not agree with today. These are areas where you could improve. What would you have to do differently for your answers to change? Some of your findings may require relatively simple fixes. Others could be extremely difficult habits or deeply ingrained mannerisms that may seem impossible to change.

The best way to approach the challenge of improvement is to prioritize your improvement opportunities and list them from simplest to most difficult to do. It could seem overwhelming to try to do everything at once, so start working on the easier areas first and develop a plan for the more challenging areas. Your objective in prioritizing these opportunities for improvement is to ensure that you are working on those things that will yield the greatest improvement in the most efficient manner.

Most importantly, give things time. Change won't happen overnight. After you have worked on your priority items for a few weeks, you should update your worksheets and review the statements of Golf MasterMind traits again and note how your answers have changed.

•   •   •

I say that becoming a Golf MasterMind Pro is not difficult, and that anyone can be one. You do not have to be a scratch golfer or an elite player to be a Golf MasterMind Pro... but being one just might make you an elite player. I'll illustrate my point with two examples. First, I had the privilege of being great friends with a man named Steve Condore. Steve and I met through golf, and became lifelong friends through our love of the game. He and I played many rounds together, with the winner earning bragging rights – and $1. We never played for more, because something more important was on the line: pride.

Steve was a low single digit handicap golfer who usually shot close to par. Steve had the smallest "gap" (refer to chapter 2) of anyone I have ever met. He was tenacious, and you could never count him out of a hole. He literally would find a way to save par from just about anywhere. He knew his game and played without ego, laying up or finding the safe play when necessary. I never saw him let anger affect his game. He was full of confidence and knew that he could play and enjoy himself with anyone at any time. We never knew it back then, but he was a Golf MasterMind Pro.

Second, I played high school golf with a young man named Murray Miller. Murray usually scored in the low 40's in our nine hole matches, but he was doggedly consistent. He never gave up, and would challenge anyone to a game. His tenacity was amazing, and like Steve, he was never out of a match. Looking back, Murray was also a Golf MasterMind Pro.

The one trait that both Steve and Murray had in common was mental toughness, probably the most important ingredient in motivation.

My point is that your goal should be to make the most of whatever game you have, every time you play. Yes, you should practice and take lessons and work to improve your physical game. This will improve your potential scores, but you may find that improvement doesn't come easily. Old habits are difficult to change, and changing motor skills takes hundreds or even thousands of repetitions.

But, you can *think differently* right now. You can make an immediate improvement in your game by following the principles outlined in this book and plotting your course to better golf as you climb the Peak Performance Pyramid. It may require that you re-think your approach to the game in some ways. You may need to reassess your skills and abilities and apply a dose of reality. You may need to refine your strategy for playing some golf courses and holes. And you may need to better manage your emotions.

Regardless, you can do it. You can be a Golf MasterMind Pro. All that is required is that you truly want to do it.

APPENDIX 1

Golf MasterMind Worksheets

- Dreams form

- Golf Goals and Objectives

- Golf MasterMind Gap Analysis Worksheet

- Golf MasterMind Skills Evaluation Worksheet

- Golf MasterMind Carry Distance Evaluation Worksheet

- Golf MasterMind Focus-Ability Worksheet

A complete set of larger worksheets and forms may be found in the Golf MasterMind Workbook, available on Amazon.com.

My dream is:

Reaching for My Dream:
My Golf MasterMind Golf Goals

_____

Goal What I want to Achieve	Objective Steps I Can Take to Achieve My Goal	By When

GOLF MASTERMIND GAP ANALYSIS WORKSHEET		Actual Score				
	Strategic Error	Tried low percentage shot				
		Unfamiliar with golf course				
		Went for green; didn't lay up				
		Went for pin instead of middle				
		Other				
	Poor Decision	Wrong club				
		Wrong target				
		Wrong line				
		Wrong option on rules situation				
		Other				
	Lack of Focus	Forgot to use preshot routine				
		Bothered by slow play				
		Bothered by another person				
		External factor (e.g., weather)				
		Lost emotional control				
		Other				
	Lack of Confidence	Wasn't sure of club				
		Had doubts about strategy				
		Didn't commit to shot				
		Didn't take my time				
		Other				
	Bad Swing	Miss right				
		Miss left				
		Poor Contact (short or long)				
		Total Gap				
		Potential Score				

Golf MasterMind Skills Evaluation Worksheet

Skill	Date	1	2	3	4	5	6	7	8	9	10	TOTAL	STANDARD
Short Putt 4 ft (max 5)													1
Long Putt 30 ft (max 10)													20
Short Chip 45 ft (max 20)													30
Long Chip 60 ft (max 20)													35
Pitch 20-25 yds (max 20)													40
Greenside Bunker (max 20)													40
Approach 40 yds (max 40)													100
Approach 60 yds (max 40)													150
Approach 80 yds (max 40)													150
Approach 100 yds (max 40)													150

Golf MasterMind Carry Distance Evaluation Worksheet

Club	Date	1	2	3	4	5	6	7	8	9	10	Average	Middle 4 Expected	Consistency Factor
EXAMPLE	9/7	145	137	128	142	133	137	141	127	140	138	137	138	6
Driver														
3-Wood														
5-Wood														
4-iron or hybrid														
5-iron														
6-iron														
7-iron														
8-iron														
9-iron														
Pitching Wedge														
Gap Wedge														
Sand Wedge														

GOLF MASTERMIND FOCUS-ABILITY SCORECARD

		1	2	3	4	5	6	7	8	9	10	11	12	13	14	15	16	17	18	Tot
Date:	Hole																			
	Par																			
Course:	Score																			
	Relation to Par																			
	Bounce-Back																			
Emotional Events	Anger																			
	Anxiety																			
	Distracted																			
	Frustrated																			
	Other																			
Time Management Skills	Pre-Shot TFA																			
	Post-Shot AFT																			

APPENDIX 2

Fun and Productive Practice Games

If you want to improve your golf game, there are no shortcuts. You must practice, and you must practice the right areas. It sounds difficult, and it is, but practice does not have to be boring! Through our extensive work teaching both juniors and adults, we have developed many fun, skill-based games that convert boring practice drills into fun activities.

Once you complete the skills evaluations and know what areas of your game you need to focus on, these games will help you sharpen your skills. Each skills area lists the games that apply to that skill. Choose one or more games from the list and you will be ready to get started lowering your scores.

In this Appendix you will find complete instructions for playing all 12 practice games. Many of the games use aiming rings that help focus on a target. These and other practice tools can be found at ParKit Golf's website (www.parkitgolf.com), along with a complete short game practice kit for seriously fun practice. Also, these 12 and many other fun practice games may be found in the ParKit Golf Encyclopedia of Fun Golf Games, available on Amazon.com.

Have fun practicing!

AIR MAIL

Air Mail is a more challenging version of "Catch Me (If You Can)." Air Mail helps develop chipping and pitching technique and distance control, and can also be used for full shots. The object is to make each ball fly farther in the air than the prior ball without going past a maximum distance boundary.

Equipment Required:

- ✓ Supply of golf balls (either regular balls or range balls)
- ✓ 2 ball markers or tees

Setup: Please refer to the drawing on the facing page.

➢ Create a starting point by placing 2 ball markers or tees 6 feet apart in an area suitable for chipping, pitching or bunker shots.

➢ Create an out-of-bounds limit so that the game will end when a ball travels beyond the limit. This could be the edge of the green, a string stretched across the green, or some other area. This limit should be about 35 yards away from the starting point.

How To Play:

➢ The goal is to hit (either a chip, pitch, or bunker shot) as many balls in a row as possible where each ball flies farther in the air than the prior ball ("target ball") without going beyond the "out-of-bounds" limit. Each ball must "air mail" the target ball.

➢ Each player begins by hitting a ball a short distance, scoring 1 point. That ball becomes the target ball for the next shot. The player then hits a second ball. If that ball flies over the target ball and stops before going out-of-bounds, score another point and that ball becomes the new target ball.

➢ If the ball lands on top of the target ball, the shot scores a point and the new target ball is whichever ball comes to rest farther from the player.

➢ Continue hitting until a ball either fails to air mail the target ball or the ball goes too far (out-of-bounds). Score a point each time the ball air mails the target ball and stays in bounds.

AIR MAIL

➢ If playing individually, keep a record of the number of points you score, and attempt to set a new record each time you play the game.

➢ If competing with multiple players, the winner is the player with the most points, once all players have had an equal number of turns.

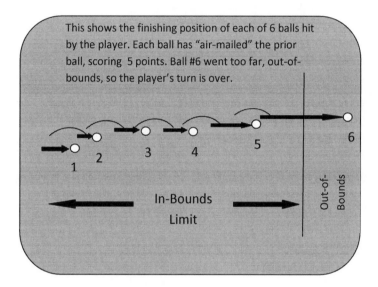

This shows the finishing position of each of 6 balls hit by the player. Each ball has "air-mailed" the prior ball, scoring 5 points. Ball #6 went too far, out-of-bounds, so the player's turn is over.

1   2   3   4   5   6

In-Bounds Limit

Out-of-Bounds

AIR MAIL

Date	Subject (circle one)	Boundary Limit Distance	Number of Points
	Chip-Pitch-Bunker-Full		
	Chip-Pitch-Bunker-Full		
	Chip-Pitch-Bunker-Full		
	Chip-Pitch-Bunker-Full		
	Chip-Pitch-Bunker-Full		
	Chip-Pitch-Bunker-Full		
	Chip-Pitch-Bunker-Full		
	Chip-Pitch-Bunker-Full		
	Chip-Pitch-Bunker-Full		
	Chip-Pitch-Bunker-Full		
	Chip-Pitch-Bunker-Full		
	Chip-Pitch-Bunker-Full		
	Chip-Pitch-Bunker-Full		
	Chip-Pitch-Bunker-Full		

AIR MAIL

Date	Subject (circle one)	Boundary Limit Distance	Number of Points
	Chip-Pitch-Bunker-Full		
	Chip-Pitch-Bunker-Full		
	Chip-Pitch-Bunker-Full		
	Chip-Pitch-Bunker-Full		
	Chip-Pitch-Bunker-Full		
	Chip-Pitch-Bunker-Full		
	Chip-Pitch-Bunker-Full		
	Chip-Pitch-Bunker-Full		
	Chip-Pitch-Bunker-Full		
	Chip-Pitch-Bunker-Full		
	Chip-Pitch-Bunker-Full		
	Chip-Pitch-Bunker-Full		
	Chip-Pitch-Bunker-Full		

BATTER UP!

Batter Up! can be used for all short game situations, and is excellent for practicing both distance and directional control. The object is to be able to repeat your swing and be able to hit each ball to the same spot on the green. You can hit it there once... can you do it again and again?

Equipment Required:

- ✓ 3' and 6' ParZone rings
- ✓ 10 golf balls, including 1 colored ball

Setup: Please refer to the drawing on the facing page.

➢ Select a flat area of the putting green away from any hole.

➢ Place the 10 balls together either on the green (if putting) or off the green (if chipping, pitching, or hitting bunker shots).

➢ Set the ParZone rings aside until all 10 balls have been hit.

How To Play:

➢ The object of the game is to achieve the highest possible "batting average" by consistently hitting the 10 balls to the same spot.

➢ Begin by hitting the colored ball toward an open area on the green (not toward a hole).

➢ Pay close attention to where this colored ball comes to rest. Then, continue hitting the nine remaining balls, trying to make each ball come to rest in the exact same place as the colored ball.

➢ After you have hit all 10 balls, select either the 3' or 6' ParZone ring and place it over the largest cluster of balls that includes the colored ball.

➢ Count the number of balls that are within the ring and multiply this number by 100; that is your "batting average."

BATTER UP!

➢ Keep a record of your batting average, and attempt to set a new record each time you play the game.

➢ If competing with multiple players, the winner is the player with the highest batting average.

➢ If the ParZone rings is too small to frequently encircle more than one ball, use the larger ring until your skill level improves.

➢ Try this game blindfolded! After hitting the first ball, close your eyes or wear a blindfold and see how well you do.

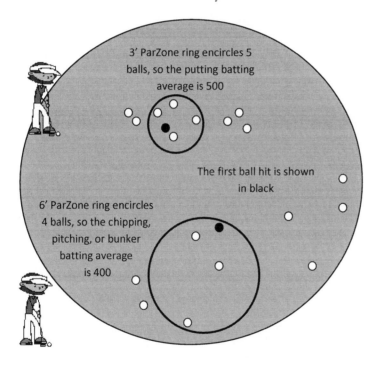

3' ParZone ring encircles 5 balls, so the putting batting average is 500

The first ball hit is shown in black

6' ParZone ring encircles 4 balls, so the chipping, pitching, or bunker batting average is 400

BATTER UP!

Date	Subject (circle one)	Ring Size (circle one)	Number of Balls In Ring
	Putt Chip Pitch Bunker	3' 6'	
	Putt Chip Pitch Bunker	3' 6'	
	Putt Chip Pitch Bunker	3' 6'	
	Putt Chip Pitch Bunker	3' 6'	
	Putt Chip Pitch Bunker	3' 6'	
	Putt Chip Pitch Bunker	3' 6'	
	Putt Chip Pitch Bunker	3' 6'	
	Putt Chip Pitch Bunker	3' 6'	
	Putt Chip Pitch Bunker	3' 6'	
	Putt Chip Pitch Bunker	3' 6'	
	Putt Chip Pitch Bunker	3' 6'	

BATTER UP!

Date	Subject (circle one)	Ring Size (circle one)		Number of Balls In Ring
	Putt Chip Pitch Bunker	3'	6'	
	Putt Chip Pitch Bunker	3'	6'	
	Putt Chip Pitch Bunker	3'	6'	
	Putt Chip Pitch Bunker	3'	6'	
	Putt Chip Pitch Bunker	3'	6'	
	Putt Chip Pitch Bunker	3'	6'	
	Putt Chip Pitch Bunker	3'	6'	
	Putt Chip Pitch Bunker	3'	6'	
	Putt Chip Pitch Bunker	3'	6'	
	Putt Chip Pitch Bunker	3'	6'	
	Putt Chip Pitch Bunker	3'	6'	

CATCH ME (IF YOU CAN)

Catch Me (If You Can) helps develop distance control for all types of shots, including putting, chipping, pitching, bunkers, and even full shots. The object is simple: hit each ball farther than the prior ball – as many times as possible.

Equipment Required:

- ✓ Supply of golf balls (either regular balls or range balls)
- ✓ 2 ball markers or tees

Setup: Please refer to the drawing on the facing page.

- ➤ Create a starting point by placing 2 ball markers or tees 6 feet apart either on the green (for putting) or in an area suitable for chipping, pitching, bunkers or full shots.

- ➤ Create an out-of-bounds limit so that the game will end when a ball travels beyond the limit. For putting, this could be the edge of the green, a string stretched across the green, or some other area. For chipping, pitching, and bunkers, this could be a line about 25 yards away from the starting point. For full shots it could be a yardage marker.

How To Play:

- ➤ The goal is to hit as many balls in a row as possible where each ball travels farther than the prior ball ("target ball") without going beyond the "out-of-bounds" limit. Each ball must "catch up to" the target ball.

- ➤ Each player begins by hitting a ball a short distance, scoring 1 point. That ball becomes the target ball for the next shot. The player then hits a second ball. If that ball catches or passes the target ball, score another point and that ball becomes the new target ball for the next shot.

- ➤ If the ball strikes the target ball, the shot scores a point and the new target ball is whichever ball comes to rest farther from the player.

CATCH ME (IF YOU CAN)

➤ Continue hitting until a ball either fails to catch the target ball or the ball goes too far (out-of-bounds). Score a point each time the ball catches or passes the target ball.

➤ If playing individually, keep a record of the number of points you score, and attempt to set a new record each time you play the game.

➤ If competing with multiple players, the winner is the player with the most points, once all players have had an equal number of turns.

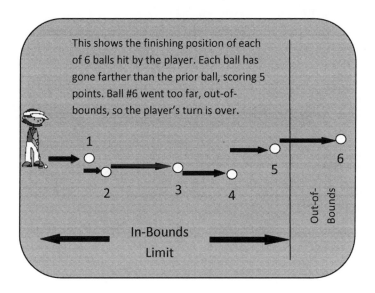

CATCH ME (IF YOU CAN)

Date	Subject (circle one)	Boundary Limit Distance	Number of Points
	Putt-Chip-Pitch-Bunker-Full		
	Putt-Chip-Pitch-Bunker-Full		
	Putt-Chip-Pitch-Bunker-Full		
	Putt-Chip-Pitch-Bunker-Full		
	Putt-Chip-Pitch-Bunker-Full		
	Putt-Chip-Pitch-Bunker-Full		
	Putt-Chip-Pitch-Bunker-Full		
	Putt-Chip-Pitch-Bunker-Full		
	Putt-Chip-Pitch-Bunker-Full		
	Putt-Chip-Pitch-Bunker-Full		
	Putt-Chip-Pitch-Bunker-Full		
	Putt-Chip-Pitch-Bunker-Full		
	Putt-Chip-Pitch-Bunker-Full		
	Putt-Chip-Pitch-Bunker-Full		

CATCH ME (IF YOU CAN)

Date	Subject (circle one)	Boundary Limit Distance	Number of Points
	Putt-Chip-Pitch-Bunker-Full		
	Putt-Chip-Pitch-Bunker-Full		
	Putt-Chip-Pitch-Bunker-Full		
	Putt-Chip-Pitch-Bunker-Full		
	Putt-Chip-Pitch-Bunker-Full		
	Putt-Chip-Pitch-Bunker-Full		
	Putt-Chip-Pitch-Bunker-Full		
	Putt-Chip-Pitch-Bunker-Full		
	Putt-Chip-Pitch-Bunker-Full		
	Putt-Chip-Pitch-Bunker-Full		
	Putt-Chip-Pitch-Bunker-Full		
	Putt-Chip-Pitch-Bunker-Full		
	Putt-Chip-Pitch-Bunker-Full		

CLOCKWORK

Clockwork is a circle putting drill that focuses on short putts (usually 2nd putts) from all angles around the hole. The object is to sink as many putts in a row as possible, working your way around the hole like the hands of a clock.

Equipment Required:

- ✓ Up to 12 golf balls
- ✓ 3' and 6' ParZone target rings

Setup: Please refer to the drawing on the facing page.

➢ For short putts, place the 6' ParZone ring around a hole on the putting green and place 6 golf balls in a circle around the hole, using the ring as a guide in placing the balls. Space the balls evenly as shown in the diagram. Remove the ring when all balls are in place.

➢ For long putts, use the 3' ParZone ring as a target instead of the hole, and place up to 12 golf balls in a circle the desired distance from the ParZone target ring (e.g. 20').

How To Play:

➢ Beginning with any ball, putt toward the hole (or ParZone ring, depending on the above setup).

➢ If the ball is holed or (for long putts) finishes in the ParZone target ring, continue putting the next ball. If the ball is not holed or does not finish within the ParZone target ring, the player's turn ends and the balls are reset for the next player or next round. Continue putting, adding more balls as necessary, until a putt misses the hole (or ParZone ring).

➢ Score one point for each ball that is either holed or finishes inside the ParZone target rings.

CLOCKWORK

➤ If playing individually, keep a record of the number of points you score, and attempt to set a new record each time you play the game.

➤ If competing with multiple players, the winner is the player with the most points, once all players have had an equal number of turns.

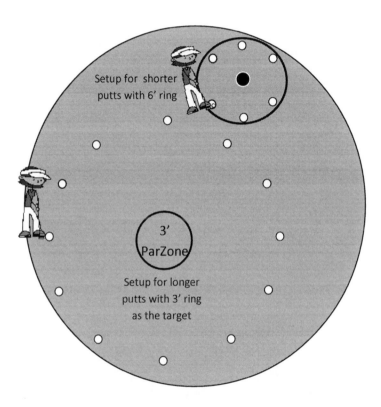

CLOCKWORK

Date	Target (circle one)	Number of Putts In A Row
	Hole 3'Ring	
	Hole 3'Ring	
	Hole 3'Ring	
	Hole 3'Ring	
	Hole 3'Ring	
	Hole 3'Ring	
	Hole 3'Ring	
	Hole 3'Ring	
	Hole 3'Ring	
	Hole 3'Ring	
	Hole 3'Ring	
	Hole 3'Ring	
	Hole 3'Ring	

CLOCKWORK

Date	Target (circle one)		Number of Putts In A Row
	Hole	3'Ring	
	Hole	3'Ring	
	Hole	3'Ring	
	Hole	3'Ring	
	Hole	3'Ring	
	Hole	3'Ring	
	Hole	3'Ring	
	Hole	3'Ring	
	Hole	3'Ring	
	Hole	3'Ring	
	Hole	3'Ring	
	Hole	3'Ring	
	Hole	3'Ring	

CLUB TRICKS

Club Tricks helps you learn that you can successfully hit a shot with many different clubs. The object is to learn to use a variety of clubs for a particular shot, and ultimately to be able to select the best club for each situation. For any given shot, you may have a choice of several clubs. You should always try to choose the easiest and most reliable club for each shot.

Equipment Required:

- ✓ 6' ParZone ring
- ✓ 12 colored golf balls – 4 each in 3 colors
- ✓ Selection of golf clubs (e.g., sand wedge, wedge, and 8-iron)

Setup: Please refer to the drawing on the facing page.

➢ Select an area of the putting green away from any hole and place the 6' ParZone ring on the green.

➢ Place the 12 balls off the green in 3 color-coded groups, each with 4 balls.

How To Play:

➢ The object of the game is to hit all 12 balls into the ParZone target ring, using three different clubs for the same shot. In doing so, you will learn how to control your ball with different clubs. You will also learn which clubs are best for certain types of shots.

➢ Begin by selecting a club and hitting the first four colored balls toward the ParZone target ring. Pay attention to how easy or difficult it is to hit the balls into the ParZone ring. Your goal is to learn which club is the easiest to use for the situation.

➢ After hitting the first four balls, select a different club and repeat the above with the next four colored balls. Using the third club, repeat again with the remaining colored balls.

CLUB TRICKS

➢ Compare the number of balls that were within the target ring for each club. Pay attention to which group of balls are the least consistent or farthest from the target ring.

➢ Replace the club that produced the worst results with a different club and repeat the entire game from the same situation.

➢ Through the process of elimination, discover the club that is the easiest to use for the situation.

➢ Keep a record of which clubs are the easiest to use in different situations.

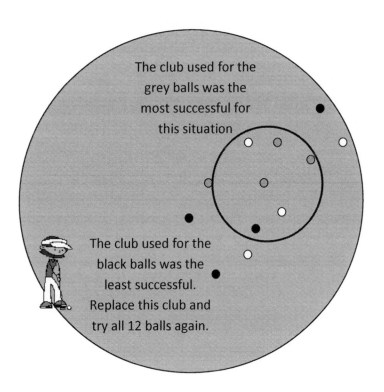

The club used for the grey balls was the most successful for this situation

The club used for the black balls was the least successful. Replace this club and try all 12 balls again.

CLUB TRICKS

Date	Describe the Situation	Best Club for Situation

CLUB TRICKS

Date	Describe the Situation	Best Club for Situation

LAGMASTER

LagMaster is a putting distance control game that focuses on both long and short putts. The object is to hole each ball in the fewest strokes possible.

Equipment Required:

- ✓ 5 balls
- ✓ 4 ball markers or tees
- ✓ 6' ParZone ring

Setup: Please refer to the drawing on the facing page.

➤ Place the 6' ParZone ring around a hole on the putting green as shown.

➤ Place the ball markers 5 feet, 10 feet, 20 feet, and 40 feet from the hole.

How To Play:

➤ Beginning with all 5 balls at the 40' marker, putt each ball toward the hole surrounded by the ParZone target ring, counting each stroke.

➤ Any ball that is holed is removed from future play.

➤ Any ball that finishes within the ParZone target ring is moved to the next closest marker.

➤ Continue putting the remaining balls from the same marker until each ball is either holed or finishes within the ParZone target ring. Remember to count each stroke.

➤ When all remaining balls have reached the closest marker (the 5' marker), remove the ParZone ring and putt the remaining balls to the hole until all of the balls are holed, continuing to count each stroke.

LAGMASTER

➢ The game is over when all 5 balls have been holed from any distance.

➢ Keep a record of the number of putts you require to hole all five balls and attempt to set a new (lower) record each time you play.

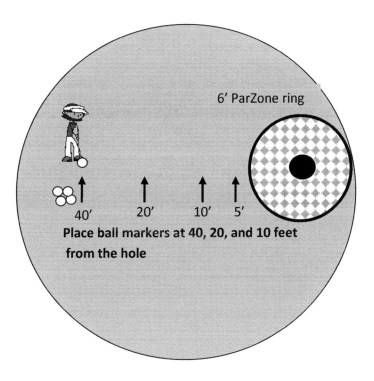

6' ParZone ring

40'   20'   10'   5'

Place ball markers at 40, 20, and 10 feet from the hole

LAGMASTER

Date	Size of ParZone ring Used (circle one)	Number of Putts Required to Hole 5 Balls
	3' 6'	
	3' 6'	
	3' 6'	
	3' 6'	
	3' 6'	
	3' 6'	
	3' 6'	
	3' 6'	
	3' 6'	
	3' 6'	
	3' 6'	
	3' 6'	
	3' 6'	

LAGMASTER

Date	Size of ParZone ring Used (circle one)		Number of Putts Required to Hole 5 Balls
	3'	6'	
	3'	6'	
	3'	6'	
	3'	6'	
	3'	6'	
	3'	6'	
	3'	6'	
	3'	6'	
	3'	6'	
	3'	6'	
	3'	6'	
	3'	6'	
	3'	6'	

LANDING ZONE

Landing Zone helps develop distance and directional control for short game shots. When hitting shots from around the green, focus on where the ball should land in order to roll to the hole. The object is to land the ball in the correct spot for chipping, pitching, and bunker shots.

Equipment Required:

- ✓ 3' and 6' ParZone rings
- ✓ 2 ball markers

Setup: Please refer to the drawing on the facing page.

➤ Place 2 ball markers or tees 6 feet apart in an area suitable for chipping, pitching or bunker shots of any length. Many setups are possible, depending on whether you are playing the game while chipping, pitching, or hitting bunker shots. Place a supply of golf balls in the station.

➤ Place the 3' or 6' ParZone ring on the green or another suitable landing place. Try to determine where the ball should land in order to roll to your target (the hole or other target).

How To Play:

➤ The object of the game is to land your ball inside the ParZone target ring as many times in a row as possible.

➤ Keep a record of the number of times in a row you are able to land a ball inside the ParZone target ring, and attempt to set a new record each time you play the game.

➤ Practice using different clubs while chipping or pitching, continuing to land the ball within the ParZone target ring. Pay close attention to where the ball ends up with different clubs.

LANDING ZONE

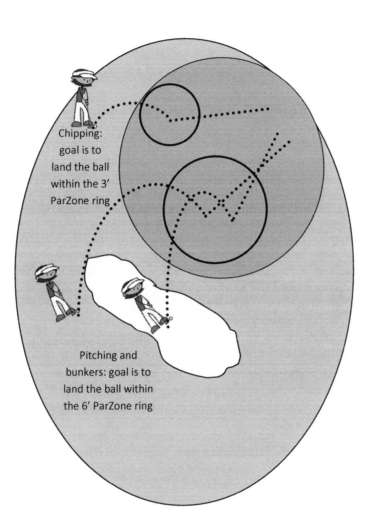

Chipping: goal is to land the ball within the 3' ParZone ring

Pitching and bunkers: goal is to land the ball within the 6' ParZone ring

LANDING ZONE

Date	Subject (circle one)	Ring Size (circle one)	Number of Balls In Ring
	Chip Pitch Bunker	3' 6'	
	Chip Pitch Bunker	3' 6'	
	Chip Pitch Bunker	3' 6'	
	Chip Pitch Bunker	3' 6'	
	Chip Pitch Bunker	3' 6'	
	Chip Pitch Bunker	3' 6'	
	Chip Pitch Bunker	3' 6'	
	Chip Pitch Bunker	3' 6'	
	Chip Pitch Bunker	3' 6'	
	Chip Pitch Bunker	3' 6'	
	Chip Pitch Bunker	3' 6'	
	Chip Pitch Bunker	3' 6'	
	Chip Pitch Bunker	3' 6'	

LANDING ZONE

Date	Subject (circle one)	Ring Size (circle one)	Number of Balls In Ring
	Chip Pitch Bunker	3' 6'	
	Chip Pitch Bunker	3' 6'	
	Chip Pitch Bunker	3' 6'	
	Chip Pitch Bunker	3' 6'	
	Chip Pitch Bunker	3' 6'	
	Chip Pitch Bunker	3' 6'	
	Chip Pitch Bunker	3' 6'	
	Chip Pitch Bunker	3' 6'	
	Chip Pitch Bunker	3' 6'	
	Chip Pitch Bunker	3' 6'	
	Chip Pitch Bunker	3' 6'	
	Chip Pitch Bunker	3' 6'	
	Chip Pitch Bunker	3' 6'	

LINE IT UP

Line It Up helps focus on putting directional control by helping you learn to roll the ball in a perfectly straight line. Line It Up is also friendly for greenskeepers who do not like chalk putting lines on the green.

Equipment Required:

- ✓ 5 golf balls
- ✓ ParKit Golf putting pins and string

Setup: Please refer to the drawing on the facing page.

➢ Find a flat portion of the putting green where you will have a straight putt. You can find a straight putt on a sloped green by making a few test rolls to the hole from different locations.

➢ Tie a 10 foot length of string to the pins and push one putting pin into the green about 3" behind the hole.

➢ Push the other putting pin into the green about 10' from the hole at the spot from which you will have a straight putt and tighten so that the string is taut. The string should be a few inches off the green.

How To Play:

➢ Place a ball directly under the string. Paying attention to the path of your club head compared to the string, putt the ball toward the hole. The ball should stay on line with the string. Continue putting until you miss, scoring a point for each holed putt.

➢ Keep a record of the number of points you score, and attempt to set a new record each time you play the game.

LINE IT UP

➤ If competing with multiple players, the winner is the player with the most points, once all players have had an equal number of turns.

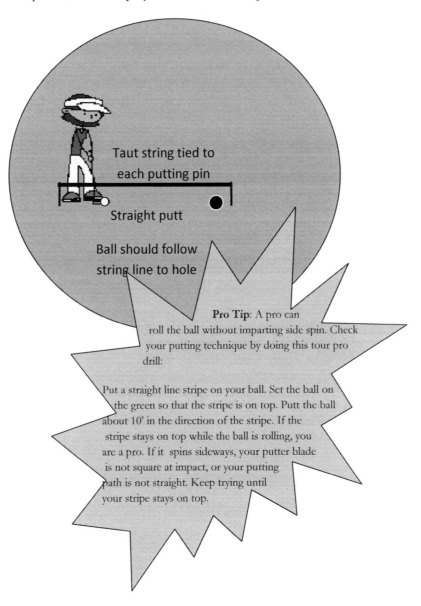

Taut string tied to each putting pin

Straight putt

Ball should follow string line to hole

Pro Tip: A pro can roll the ball without imparting side spin. Check your putting technique by doing this tour pro drill:

Put a straight line stripe on your ball. Set the ball on the green so that the stripe is on top. Putt the ball about 10' in the direction of the stripe. If the stripe stays on top while the ball is rolling, you are a pro. If it spins sideways, your putter blade is not square at impact, or your putting path is not straight. Keep trying until your stripe stays on top.

LINE IT UP

Date	Estimated Distance From Hole	Number of Putts In A Row

LINE IT UP

Date	Estimated Distance From Hole	Number of Putts In A Row

SCHOOL

School is a ladder putting drill that helps develop distance control. The object is to roll the ball either into the hole or so that it stops within a close distance just past he hole. If successful, you "graduate" to the next grade and try again from farther away.

Equipment Required:

- ✓ 5 or more ball markers (either coins or tees work well)
- ✓ 3-foot ParZone ring

Setup: Please refer to the drawing on the facing page.

➢ Create a "passing zone" by placing the 3-foot ParZone ring around the hole as shown. The passing zone begins at the hole and includes the area within the ParZone target ring.

➢ Beginning a short distance from the hole, place the ball markers at 3-foot increments moving away from the hole. Use your judgment on the spacing of the markers. For beginners, keep the markers closer together. For advanced players, spread them farther apart.

➢ The closest marker represents "1st grade", the next marker "2nd grade", then "3rd grade", and so on.

How To Play:

➢ Beginning at "1st grade," putt toward the hole.

➢ If the ball is holed or finishes inside the "passing zone" the player advances to the next grade and putts again.

➢ If the ball does not finish either in the hole or within the passing zone, the player goes back to 1st grade.

➢ If it becomes too easy to reach the highest grade, spread the grade markers farther apart or use a breaking putt.

➢ If playing individually, keep a record of the number of putts you require to reach the highest grade and attempt to set a new (lower) record each time you play.

➢ If competing with multiple players, the winner is the only player to reach the highest grade, once all players have had an equal number of turns (i.e., when a player reaches the end, any remaining players after him in the round get a chance to tie). In the event of a tie, continue adding grades farther from the hole until only one person passes.

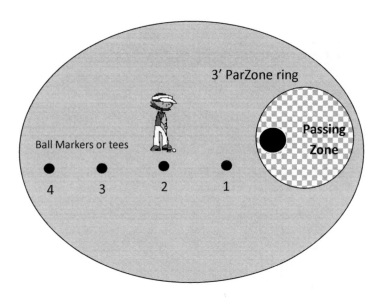

SCHOOL

Date	Grade Reached (circle one)	# Putts Required to Reach Final Grade
	1 2 3 4 5 6 7 8 9	
	1 2 3 4 5 6 7 8 9	
	1 2 3 4 5 6 7 8 9	
	1 2 3 4 5 6 7 8 9	
	1 2 3 4 5 6 7 8 9	
	1 2 3 4 5 6 7 8 9	
	1 2 3 4 5 6 7 8 9	
	1 2 3 4 5 6 7 8 9	
	1 2 3 4 5 6 7 8 9	
	1 2 3 4 5 6 7 8 9	
	1 2 3 4 5 6 7 8 9	
	1 2 3 4 5 6 7 8 9	
	1 2 3 4 5 6 7 8 9	

SCHOOL

Date	Grade Reached (circle one)	# Putts Required to Reach Final Grade
	1 2 3 4 5 6 7 8 9	
	1 2 3 4 5 6 7 8 9	
	1 2 3 4 5 6 7 8 9	
	1 2 3 4 5 6 7 8 9	
	1 2 3 4 5 6 7 8 9	
	1 2 3 4 5 6 7 8 9	
	1 2 3 4 5 6 7 8 9	
	1 2 3 4 5 6 7 8 9	
	1 2 3 4 5 6 7 8 9	
	1 2 3 4 5 6 7 8 9	
	1 2 3 4 5 6 7 8 9	
	1 2 3 4 5 6 7 8 9	
	1 2 3 4 5 6 7 8 9	

SEQUENCE

Sequence tests your ability to repeatedly hit good shots with any club, and helps develop consistent shotmaking technique and performance under pressure.

Equipment Required:

- ✓ Supply of golf balls (either regular balls or range balls)
- ✓ ParZone ring (size determined by skill level)
- ✓ 2 ball markers or tees

Setup: Please refer to the drawing on the facing page.

➢ Create a starting point by placing 2 ball markers or tees 6 feet apart either on the green (for putting) or in an area suitable for chipping, pitching or bunker shots of any length. Many setups are possible, depending on whether you are playing the game while putting, chipping, pitching, bunker, or full shots.

➢ Depending on whether you are playing Sequence with putting, chipping, pitching, bunker, or full shots, you must create a target goal. This could be the hole, any size ring, or a even a practice green, depending upon your personal standard of an acceptable shot. The goal should be set so that it is challenging, but still reasonably achievable.

How To Play:

➢ The object of the game is to hit as many consecutive balls into your target as possible.

➢ Define your goal for the situation. For shorter putts, it might be the hole. For longer putts, it may be to putt the ball into the 3' ParZone ring. For chip, pitch, or standard bunker shots, it may be to stop the ball within the 6' ParZone ring. For difficult bunker shots, it may be to stop the ball on the green.

➢ Begin hitting shots toward your goal. If you succeed (as defined above), continue until you fail to achieve your goal.

SEQUENCE

> ➢ Each ball that scores a goal counts as one point. The game (or your turn) ends when you fail to score a goal.

> ➢ Keep a record of the number of points you score, and attempt to set a new record each time you play the game.

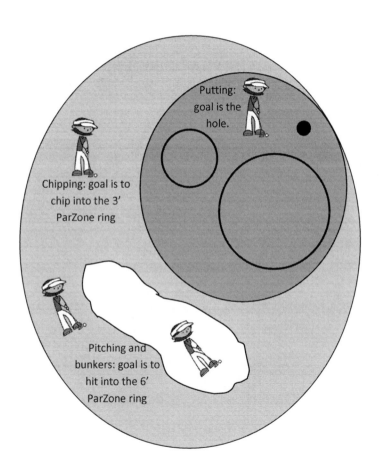

SEQUENCE

Date	Subject (circle one)	Goal (circle one)		No. of Points
	Putt Chip Pitch Bunker Full	In Ring On Hole 3' 6' Green		
	Putt Chip Pitch Bunker Full	In Ring On Hole 3' 6' Green		
	Putt Chip Pitch Bunker Full	In Ring On Hole 3' 6' Green		
	Putt Chip Pitch Bunker Full	In Ring On Hole 3' 6' Green		
	Putt Chip Pitch Bunker Full	In Ring On Hole 3' 6' Green		
	Putt Chip Pitch Bunker Full	In Ring On Hole 3' 6' Green		
	Putt Chip Pitch Bunker Full	In Ring On Hole 3' 6' Green		
	Putt Chip Pitch Bunker Full	In Ring On Hole 3' 6' Green		
	Putt Chip Pitch Bunker Full	In Ring On Hole 3' 6' Green		
	Putt Chip Pitch Bunker Full	In Ring On Hole 3' 6' Green		
	Putt Chip Pitch Bunker Full	In Ring On Hole 3' 6' Green		

SEQUENCE

Date	Subject (circle one)	Goal (circle one)		No. of Points
	Putt Chip Pitch Bunker Full	In Hole	Ring 3' 6'	On Green
	Putt Chip Pitch Bunker Full	In Hole	Ring 3' 6'	On Green
	Putt Chip Pitch Bunker Full	In Hole	Ring 3' 6'	On Green
	Putt Chip Pitch Bunker Full	In Hole	Ring 3' 6'	On Green
	Putt Chip Pitch Bunker Full	In Hole	Ring 3' 6'	On Green
	Putt Chip Pitch Bunker Full	In Hole	Ring 3' 6'	On Green
	Putt Chip Pitch Bunker Full	In Hole	Ring 3' 6'	On Green
	Putt Chip Pitch Bunker Full	In Hole	Ring 3' 6'	On Green
	Putt Chip Pitch Bunker Full	In Hole	Ring 3' 6'	On Green
	Putt Chip Pitch Bunker Full	In Hole	Ring 3' 6'	On Green
	Putt Chip Pitch Bunker Full	In Hole	Ring 3' 6'	On Green

SNEAK ATTACK

Sneak Attack is the opposite of "Catch Me (If You Can)," and helps develop distance control and feel for all types of shots, including putting, chipping, pitching, bunkers, and even full shots. The object is simple: hit each ball as close as possible to the prior ball without going past – in other words, "sneak up" on the prior ball..

Equipment Required:

- ✓ Supply of golf balls (either regular balls or range balls)
- ✓ 2 ball markers or tees

Setup: Please refer to the drawing on the facing page.

➢ Create a starting point by placing 2 ball markers or tees 6 feet apart either on the green (for putting) or in an area suitable for chipping, pitching, bunkers or full shots.

➢ Create an out-of-bounds limit or maximum distance that the first ball can travel. For putting, this could be the edge of the green, a string stretched across the green, or some other area. For chipping, pitching, and bunkers, this could be a line about 25 yards away from the starting point. For full shots it could be a yardage marker.

How To Play:

➢ The goal is to hit as many balls in a row as possible where no ball travels farther than the prior ball ("target ball"). Each ball must "sneak up" on the target ball.

➢ Begin by hitting the first ball as far as possible, without going over the out-of-bounds limit. That ball becomes the target ball for the next shot.

➢ Hit each subsequent ball, trying to come as close as possible to the prior ball. Each ball that stops short of the prior ball scores a point and that ball becomes the new target ball for the next shot.

SNEAK ATTACK

> ➤ If a ball touches or goes farther than the target ball, the game ends.

> ➤ Continue hitting until a ball either touches the target ball or goes farther than the target ball. Score a point each time the ball stops short of the target ball.

> ➤ If playing individually, keep a record of the number of points you score, and attempt to set a new record each time you play the game.

> ➤ If competing with multiple players, the winner is the player with the most points, once all players have had an equal number of turns.

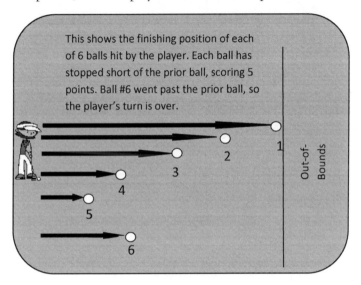

This shows the finishing position of each of 6 balls hit by the player. Each ball has stopped short of the prior ball, scoring 5 points. Ball #6 went past the prior ball, so the player's turn is over.

SNEAK ATTACK

Date	Subject (circle one)	Boundary Limit Distance	Number of Points
	Putt-Chip-Pitch-Bunker		
	Putt-Chip-Pitch-Bunker		
	Putt-Chip-Pitch-Bunker		
	Putt-Chip-Pitch-Bunker		
	Putt-Chip-Pitch-Bunker		
	Putt-Chip-Pitch-Bunker		
	Putt-Chip-Pitch-Bunker		
	Putt-Chip-Pitch-Bunker		
	Putt-Chip-Pitch-Bunker		
	Putt-Chip-Pitch-Bunker		
	Putt-Chip-Pitch-Bunker		
	Putt-Chip-Pitch-Bunker		
	Putt-Chip-Pitch-Bunker		
	Putt-Chip-Pitch-Bunker		

SNEAK ATTACK

Date	Subject (circle one)	Boundary Limit Distance	Number of Points
	Putt-Chip-Pitch-Bunker		
	Putt-Chip-Pitch-Bunker		
	Putt-Chip-Pitch-Bunker		
	Putt-Chip-Pitch-Bunker		
	Putt-Chip-Pitch-Bunker		
	Putt-Chip-Pitch-Bunker		
	Putt-Chip-Pitch-Bunker		
	Putt-Chip-Pitch-Bunker		
	Putt-Chip-Pitch-Bunker		
	Putt-Chip-Pitch-Bunker		
	Putt-Chip-Pitch-Bunker		
	Putt-Chip-Pitch-Bunker		

WICKET TRAIL

Wicket Trail helps visualize breaks, or slopes, on the green and helps understand how putts break. The object is to arrange wickets on the green so that you can putt through them to the hole.

Equipment Required:

- ✓ 5 ParKit Golf Wickets (large 1 point wickets)
- ✓ 2 ball markers

Setup: Please refer to the drawing on the facing page.

➢ Choose a spot on the practice putting green with some slope that will produce a breaking putt.

➢ Place the two ball markers about 6" apart on the green, about 10 feet away from the hole. Place your ball between the markers.

➢ Survey the putt and estimate the curvature of the putt. Mark your expected putting line by inserting each wicket into the putting green. Arrange the wickets in a curved line representing the line you think your ball must follow to reach the hole.

How To Play:

➢ The object of the game is to putt your ball through all five wickets and into the hole in the least number of tries.

➢ Begin by putting from between the ball markers toward the first wicket with enough speed to reach the hole.

➢ If your ball goes through each wicket and into the hole, the game is over. If the ball does not go through each wicket, try the putt again, and reset the wickets as needed. Use your best judgment of the line of the putt to reset only those wickets that need to be moved in order to mark the line of the putt to the hole.

➢ If the game seems too easy, start farther from the hole or select a putt across a more severe slope.

WICKET TRAIL

➤ Keep a record of the number of tries you require to make the putt while passing through each wicket, and attempt to set a new record each time you play the game.

➤ If competing with multiple players, the winner is the first player to hole the putt while passing through each wicket.

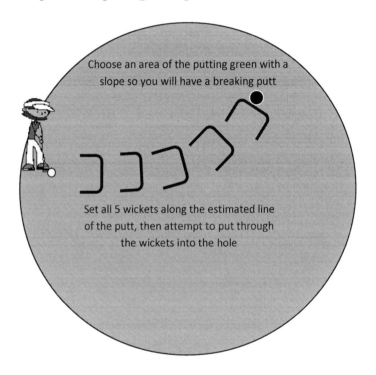

Choose an area of the putting green with a slope so you will have a breaking putt

Set all 5 wickets along the estimated line of the putt, then attempt to put through the wickets into the hole

WICKET TRAIL

Date	Estimated Distance From Hole	Number of Tries Before Holing Putt

WICKET TRAIL

Date	Estimated Distance From Hole	Number of Tries Before Holing Putt

About the Author

Rick Heard is a PGA teaching professional and co-owner of the Don Law Golf Academy in Boca Raton, Florida. He is a U.S. Kids Top 50 Master Kids Teacher, a U.S. Kids Certified Instructor, and a Certified HeartMath Coach/Mentor. He is also a co-founder of ParKit Golf, which creates innovative teaching tools and materials to make junior golf instruction both fun and educational.

Rick was president of the Southeast Chapter of the South Florida PGA section for six years ending in 2012, and was awarded the Chapter's Golf Professional of the Year award for 2010, in addition to the Southeast Chapter PGA Horton Smith Education Award (2007 and 2008) and the Southeast Chapter PGA Junior Leader Award (2002).

Rick's other books include "Daddy Caddy on the Bag," a book to help parents manage the complex roles of being a parent, coach and caddy for their children, "Daddy Caddy Off the Bag," to help kids learn to be independent and responsible golfers, the "ParKit Golf Encyclopedia of Fun Golf Games," the "ParKit Golf Skills Improvement Workbook," and the "ParKit Golf Book of Fun Games for Kids."

Prior to becoming a PGA golf professional, Rick enjoyed a 22-year business career in research, computer programming, technical writing, and marketing. He resides in Boca Raton, Florida with his wife Diane and their son Alex, an elite young golfer.